Against the Double Blackmail

Against the Double Blackmail

Refugees, Terror and Other Troubles with the Neighbours

SLAVOJ ŽIŽEK

ALLEN LANE
an imprint of
PENGUIN BOOKS

ALLEN LANE

UK | USA | Canada | Ireland | Australia
India | New Zealand | South Africa

Allen Lane is part of the Penguin Random House group of companies
whose addresses can be found at global.penguinrandomhouse.com.

First published 2016
003

Copyright © Slavoj Žižek, 2016

The moral right of the author has been asserted

Set in 12.5/14.75 pt Garamond MT Std
Typeset by Jouve (UK), Milton Keynes
Printed in Great Britain by Clays Ltd, St Ives plc

A CIP catalogue record for this book is available from the British Library

ISBN: 978-0-241-27884-0

www.greenpenguin.co.uk

For Jela, till death (of our enemies, not ours)!

Contents

The Double Blackmail

In her classic study *On Death and Dying*, Elisabeth Kübler-Ross sets out her now-famous description of how we react to the news that we have a terminal illness. Our response evolves over five stages: *denial* (we simply refuse to accept the fact: 'This can't be happening, not to me'); *anger* (which explodes when we can no longer deny the fact: 'How can this be happening to me?'); *bargaining* (the hope we can somehow postpone or diminish the fact: 'Just let me live to see my children graduate'); *depression* (libidinal disinvestment: 'I'm going to die, so why bother with anything?'); *acceptance* ('I can't fight it; I may as well prepare for it'). Kübler-Ross applied these stages to any form of catastrophic personal loss (joblessness, death of a loved one, divorce, drug addiction); she also emphasized that they do not necessarily come in the same order, nor are all five stages always experienced.

In Western Europe today, the reaction of both authorities and public opinion to the flow of refugees from Africa and the Middle East seems to comprise a similar combination of disparate reactions. There is – less and less – denial: 'It's not so serious, let's just ignore it.' There is anger: 'Refugees are a threat to our way of life – and besides, radical Islamists hide among them. They should be stopped at all costs!' There is bargaining: 'OK, let's establish quotas and support refugee camps in their own countries!' There is depression: 'We are lost, Europe is turning into Europastan!' What is entirely lacking among these responses, though, is the last of Kübler-Ross's stages: acceptance, which, in this case, means a consistent Europe-wide plan of how to deal with the refugee issue.

The terrorist attacks across Paris in November 2015 complicated matters still further. Of course, the atrocities should be unconditionally condemned, but – this 'but' doesn't usher in any mitigating circumstances; there can be none – but it is just that they need to be *really* condemned. What such a condemnation needs is more than what is usually portrayed in the media, the simple, pathetic spectacle of the solidarity of all of us (free, democratic, civilized people) against the murderous Islamic Monster. There is something weird about the solemn declarations that we are at war with the Islamic State: all the world's superpowers against a religious gang controlling a small patch of mostly desert land ... This doesn't mean, of course, that we should not focus on destroying ISIS, unconditionally, with no 'but'. The only 'but' is that we should *really* focus on destroying it. In order to bring about this destruction, much more is needed than the pathetic declarations and appeals to the solidarity of all 'civilized' forces against the demonized fundamentalist enemy. What we must avoid doing is engaging in the usual Left-liberal litany of 'One cannot fight terror with terror, violence only breeds more violence.' Now is the time to start raising unpleasant questions: how is it possible for Islamic State to exist, to survive? We all know, in spite of the formal condemnation and rejection from all sides, there are forces and states that silently not only tolerate it, but help it.

As David Graeber pointed out recently, had Turkey placed the same kind of absolute blockade on ISIS territories as they have done on Kurdish-held parts of Syria, and shown the same sort of 'benign neglect' towards the PKK and YPG that they have been offering to Islamic State, Islamic State would long since have collapsed, and the Paris attacks would probably not have happened.[1] Similar things are going on elsewhere in the region: Saudi Arabia, the US's key ally, welcomes ISIS's war on Shia Islam, and even Israel is suspiciously half-hearted in its condemnation of ISIS out of opportunistic calculation (ISIS is fighting the pro-Iranian Shia forces, which Israel considers its main enemy).

The deal on refugees between the EU and Turkey, announced at the end of November 2015 – Turkey will curb the flow of refugees into Europe in exchange for generous financial help, initially of 3 billion Euro – is a shamelessly disgusting act, a proper ethico-political catastrophe. Is this how the 'war on terror' is to be conducted, by succumbing to the Turkish blackmail and rewarding one of the main culprits of the rise of ISIS in Syria? The opportunistic-pragmatic justification of this deal is clear (bribing Turkey is the most obvious way to limit the flow of refugees), but the long-term consequences will be catastrophic.

This obscure background makes it evident that the 'total war' against ISIS should not be taken seriously – the big warriors don't really mean it. We are definitely in the midst of the clash of civilizations (the Christian West versus radicalized Islam), but in fact there are clashes within each civilization: in the Christian space, it is the US and Western Europe against Russia; in the Muslim space it is Sunnis against Shias. The monstrosity of ISIS serves as a fetish covering all these struggles, in which every side pretends to fight ISIS in order to hit its true enemy.

The first thing we should note in a more serious analysis that reaches beyond the clichés of the 'war on terror' is that the Paris attacks were a momentary brutal disruption of normal everyday life. (Significantly, of course, the attacks focused not on the Western military or political establishments, but on symbols of everyday popular culture – restaurants, rock venues, football stadiums.) This form of terrorism – a momentary disturbance – tends to characterize attacks on developed Western countries, in clear contrast to many countries across the developing world, where violence is a permanent fact of life. Think about daily life in Congo, Afghanistan, Syria, Iraq, Lebanon . . . where are the outpourings of international solidarity in the face of the constant atrocities perpetrated there? We should remember *now* that we live in a kind of glasshouse, in which terrorist violence for the most part exists in the public imagination as a threat, which explodes intermittently, in contrast to countries where – usually with the participation or complicity of the West – daily life consists of more or less uninterrupted terror and brutality.

In *In the World Interior of Capital*, Peter Sloterdijk demonstrates how, through the processes of globalization, the capitalist system has come to determine all conditions of life. One of the first major signs of this stage of development came with the building of London's Crystal Palace, the site of the first world exhibition in 1851. Here was a tangible example of the inevitable exclusivity of globalization, as the construction and expansion of a world interior whose invisible boundaries are nevertheless virtually insurmountable from without, and which, now, is inhabited by the one and a half billion 'winners' of globalization; three times this number are left standing outside the door. Consequently, as Sloterdijk puts it, 'the world interior of capital is not an *agora* or a trade fair beneath the open sky, but rather a hothouse that has drawn inwards everything that was once on the outside.'[2] This interior, built on capitalist excesses, determines everything: 'The primary fact of the Modern Age was not that the earth goes around the sun, but that money goes around the earth.'[3] After the process that transformed the world into the globe, 'social life could only take place in an expanded interior, a domestically and artificially climatized inner space.'[4] Now, with the complete dominance of cultural capitalism, all potentially world-system-changing upheavals are contained: 'No more historic events could take place under such conditions' – now, any such disruptions can be 'at most, domestic accidents.'[5]

What Sloterdijk correctly points out is that capitalist globalization stands not only for openness and conquest, but also for the idea of a self-enclosed globe separating its privileged Inside from its Outside. These two aspects of globalization are inseparable: capitalism's global reach is grounded in the way it introduces a radical class division across the entire globe, separating those protected by the sphere from those left vulnerable outside it.

In this way, both the Paris terrorist attacks and the now constant flow of refugees into Europe are momentary reminders of the violent world outside our glasshouse: a world which, for us insiders, appears mostly on TV and in media reports about distant conflicts, not as part of our everyday reality. That's why it is our duty to become fully aware of the brutal violence that pervades the world outside our protected environment – violence that is not only religious, ethnic and political but also sexual. In her outstanding analysis of the trial of South African athlete Oscar Pistorius, Jacqueline Rose pointed out how Pistorius's killing of his girlfriend Reeva Steenkamp has to be read against both the complex background of white men's fear of black violence and the terrible reality of widespread violence against women: 'Every four minutes in South Africa a woman or a girl – often a teenager, sometimes a child – is reported raped and every eight hours a woman is killed by her partner. The phenomenon has a name in South Africa: "intimate femicide", or, as the journalist and crime writer Margie Orford calls the repeated killing of women across the country, "serial femicide".'[6]

This violence against women should in no way be dismissed as marginal. Today, anti-colonialist critiques of the West – from such disparate sources as the Nigerian radical Islamist group Boko Haram, to Zimbabwe's Robert Mugabe to Vladimir Putin – manifest themselves increasingly in the rejection of what they term Western sexual confusion, and as a demand for returning to a 'traditional' sexual hierarchy. I am, of course, well aware that the export of Western feminism and individual human rights can serve as a tool of ideological and economic neocolonialism (we all remember how some American feminists supported the US intervention in Iraq as a way to 'liberate' women there: the result, as we know now, has been exactly the opposite[7]). But one should nonetheless absolutely reject drawing from this the conclusion that Western Leftists should make some kind of 'strategic compromise' in which the humiliation and persecution of women and gays are silently tolerated on behalf of the 'greater' anti-imperialist struggle.

So, what to do with hundreds of thousands of people who, desperate to escape war and hunger, wait in north Africa or on the shores of Syria, trying to cross the Mediterranean to find refuge in Europe? Two main answers present themselves, two versions of ideological blackmail, which make us irreparably guilty. Left liberals, expressing their outrage at how Europe is allowing thousands to drown in the Mediterranean, state that Europe should show solidarity, should open its doors widely. Anti-immigrant populists, on the other hand, claim that we should protect our way of life, pull up the drawbridge and let Africans or Arabs solve their own problems. Both solutions are bad, but which is worse? To paraphrase Stalin, they are both worse.

The greatest hypocrites are those who advocate open borders: secretly, they know very well this will never happen, for it would trigger an instant populist revolt in Europe. They play the Beautiful Soul, which feels superior to the corrupted world while secretly participating in it: they need this corrupted world as the only terrain where they can exert their moral superiority. The reason why these appeals to our empathy towards the poor refugees flowing into Europe are not enough was formulated a century ago by Oscar Wilde in the opening lines of *The Soul of Man Under Socialism*. There, he pointed out that 'it is much more easy to have sympathy with suffering than it is to have sympathy with thought':

> [People] find themselves surrounded by hideous poverty, by hideous ugliness, by hideous starvation. It is inevitable that they should be strongly moved by all this . . . Accordingly, with admirable though misdirected intentions, they very seriously and very sentimentally set themselves to the task of remedying the evils that they see. But their remedies do not cure the disease: they merely prolong it. Indeed, their remedies are part of the disease. They try to solve the problem of poverty, for instance, by keeping the poor alive; or, in the case of a very advanced school, by amusing the poor. But this is not a solution: it is an aggravation of the difficulty. The proper aim is to try and reconstruct society on such a basis that poverty will be impossible. And the altruistic virtues have really prevented the carrying out of this aim.[8]

With regard to the refugees, our proper aim should be to try and reconstruct global society on such a basis that desperate refugees will no longer be forced to wander around. Utopian as it may appear, this large-scale solution is the only realist one, and the display of altruistic virtues ultimately prevents the carrying out of this aim. The more we treat refugees as objects of humanitarian help, and allow the situation which compelled them to leave their countries to prevail, the more they come to Europe, until tensions reach boiling point, not only in the refugees' countries of origin but here as well. So, confronted with this double blackmail, we are back at the great Leninist question: what is to be done?

A Descent into the Maelstrom

The refugee crisis offers to Europe a unique chance to redefine itself, to mark its distinction from both poles that oppose it: Anglo-Saxon neoliberalism and the 'Asian values'-infused authoritarian capitalism. Those who bemoan the ongoing decline of the European Union seem to idealize its past – yet the 'democratic' EU, whose loss they now regret, never in fact existed. Recent EU policy is just a desperate attempt to make Europe fit for the new global capitalism. The usual Left-liberal critique of the EU – it's basically OK, just with something of a 'democratic deficit' – betrays the same naivety as the critics of ex-Communist countries who basically supported them while complaining about the lack of democracy. In both cases, however, these friendly critics failed to realize that the 'democratic deficit' was a necessary, inbuilt part of the structure.

But I am here even more of a sceptical pessimist. When I was recently answering questions from the readers of *Süddeutsche Zeitung* about the refugee crisis, the question that attracted by far the most attention concerned precisely democracy, but with a Rightist-populist twist: when Angela Merkel made her famous public appeal inviting hundreds of thousands into Germany, what was her democratic legitimization? What gave her the right to bring such a radical change to German life without democratic consultation? My point here, of course, is not to support anti-immigrant populists, but to clearly point out the limits of democratic legitimization. The same goes for those who advocate a radical opening of the borders: are they aware that, since our democracies are nation-state democracies, their demand equals a suspension of democracy – a gigantic and fundamental transformation should be allowed to affect a country without the democratic consultation of its population? (The answer could have been, of course, that refugees should also be given the right to vote – but this is clearly not enough, since this is a measure that can only happen after refugees have been integrated into the political system of a country.) A similar problem arises with calls for transparency in EU decisions: what I fear, for example, is that, since in many countries a majority of the public had no desire to come to Greece's aid, rendering EU negotiations public would make representatives of these countries advocate even tougher measures against Greece . . . We encounter here the old problem: what happens to democracy when the majority is inclined to vote for, say, racist and sexist laws? I am not afraid to draw the conclusion that emancipatory politics should not be bound a priori by formal-democratic procedures of legitimization. No, people quite often do *not* know what they want, or do not want what they know, or they simply want the wrong thing. There is no short-cut here.

Where, then, is Europe today? Lying in the great pincers that comprise America on the one side and China on the other. America and China, seen metaphysically, are both the same: the same hopeless frenzy of unchained technology and of the rootless organization of the average man. When the farthest corner of the globe has been conquered technologically and can be exploited economically; when any incident you like, in any place you like, at any time you like, becomes accessible as fast as you like; when, through live media coverage, you can simultaneously 'experience' a battle in the Iraqi desert and an opera performance in Beijing; when, in a global digital network, time is nothing but speed, instantaneity and simultaneity; when a winner in a reality TV show counts as the great man of a people; then, yes, there still looms like a spectre over all this uproar the question: what for? – where to? – and what then?

Everybody acquainted with Heidegger's *Introduction to Metaphysics* (*Einführung in die Metaphysik*) will easily recognize in this paragraph an ironic paraphrase of his diagnosis of the European situation in the mid 1930s. Today, there is a need among us Europeans for what Heidegger called *Auseinandersetzung* ('interpretive confrontation') with non-European others as well as with Europe's own past, in all its scope, from its Ancient and Judeo-Christian roots to the recently deceased idea of the welfare state. Today, Europe is split between the so-called Anglo-Saxon model – accept the idea of 'modernization' (shorthand for adaptation to the rules of the new global order) – and the French-German model, which is to preserve as much as possible of the 'old European' post-war welfare state. Although opposed, these options are in fact two sides of the same coin, which is why our goal should be neither to return to any idealized form of the past – both these models are clearly exhausted – nor to convince ourselves, as Europeans, that, if we are to survive as a world power, we should accommodate ourselves as fast as possible to the recent trends of globalization (which, in any case, Europe is already doing). Nor should our task be to bring about what is arguably the worst option, a 'creative synthesis' between European traditions and globalization, with the aim of achieving something one is tempted to call 'globalization with a European face'.

Every crisis is in itself the instigation of a new beginning, every failure of short-term pragmatic measures (for example, of the financial reorganization of the European Union) a blessing in disguise, an opportunity to rethink our very foundations. What we need is a *Wiederholung*, a 'retrieval-through-repetition': through a critical engagement with the entire European tradition, one should repeat the question, 'What is Europe?', or, rather, 'What does it mean for us to be Europeans?', and, in doing so, formulate a new vision. The task is a difficult one. It compels us to take the great risk of stepping into the unknown – yet its only alternative is slow decay, in which the administrators of the European Union eagerly participate.

Sometimes, faces become symbols: not symbols of the strong individuality of their bearers, but of the anonymous forces behind them. Was not the stupidly smiling Jeroen Dijsselbloem, president of the Eurogroup, the symbol of the EU's brutal pressure on Greece? Recently, the international trade deal TTIP (Transatlantic Trade and Investment Partnership) acquired a new symbol: the cold response of EU trade commissioner Cecilia Malmström who, when asked by a journalist how she could continue her promotion of TTIP in the face of massive public opposition, responded without shame: 'I do not take my mandate from the European people.'[9] In an unsurpassable act of irony, her family name is a variation of 'maelstrom'.

The general picture of TTIP's social impact is clear enough: it stands for nothing less than a brutal assault on democracy. Nowhere is this clearer than in the case of the so-called Investor–State Dispute Settlement (ISDS), which allows companies to sue governments if those governments' policies result in a loss of profits. This means, simply put, that unelected transnational corporations can dictate the policies of democratically elected governments. ISDSs are already in place in some bilateral trade agreements, so we can see how they work. The Swedish energy company Vattenfall is currently suing the German government for billions of dollars over its decision to phase out nuclear power plants in the wake of the Fukushima disaster. A public-health policy put into place by a democratically elected government is therefore being threatened by an energy giant because of a potential loss of profits. But let us forget for a moment this overall picture and focus on a more specific question: what will TTIP mean for European cultural production?

In Edgar Allan Poe's 1841 story 'A Descent into the Maelström', the narrator recounts how, shipwrecked, he avoided being sucked into a gigantic whirlpool. He remembers the phenomenon vividly: how the larger the bodies that were sucked into it, the more rapid their descent, and that spherical objects were pulled in the fastest. Seeing all this, he abandoned his ship and held on to a cylindrical barrel until he was saved several hours later.

Do proponents of so-called 'cultural exception' not envisage something similar? While our big economic companies get sucked into the vortex of the global market, perhaps we can save marginal 'light' cultural products. How? By exempting cultural products from free-market rules: allowing states to support their artistic production (with state subsidies, lower taxes, etc.), even if this means 'unfair competition' with other countries. France, for instance, insists that this is the only way for its national cinema to survive the onslaught of Hollywood blockbusters.

Can this exceptionalism work? While such measures can play a limited positive role, I see two problems. First, in today's global capitalism, culture is no longer just an exception, a kind of fragile superstructure rising above the 'real' economic infrastructure, but, more and more, a central ingredient of our mainstream 'real' economy. More than a decade ago, Jeremy Rifkin designated this new stage in our economy 'cultural capitalism'.[10] The defining feature of 'postmodern' capitalism is the direct commodification of our experience itself. Less and less are we buying products (material objects) that we want to own; increasingly, we buy life experiences, experiences of sex, eating, communicating, cultural consumption. In doing so, we are participating in a lifestyle – or, as Mark Slouka puts it succinctly, 'we become the consumers of our own lives.'[11] We no longer buy objects, we ultimately buy (the time of) our own life. In this way, Michel Foucault's notion of turning one's Self itself into a work of art gets an unexpected confirmation: I buy my bodily fitness by way of visiting fitness clubs; I buy my spiritual enlightenment by way of enrolling in courses of transcendental meditation; I buy the satisfactory self-experience of myself as ecologically aware by purchasing only organic fruit; and so on.

Second problem: even if Europe succeeds in imposing 'cultural exceptions' onto TTIP, what kind of Europe will survive the rule of TTIP? The question is therefore not whether European culture can survive TTIP, but what TTIP will do to our economy. Will Europe not slowly become what Ancient Greece was for imperial Rome: a preferred place for American and Chinese tourists, a destination for nostalgic cultural tourism with no effective relevance in the world?

Breaking the Taboos of the Left

In order to retrieve the emancipatory core of the idea of Europe, there is a whole series of Leftist taboos – attitudes that render topics untouchable, better left undisturbed – that we will have to leave behind. The first is an utter fatuity masquerading as a deep wisdom: 'An enemy is someone whose story you have not heard.'[12] There is no better literary example of this idea than Mary Shelley's *Frankenstein*. In it, Shelley does something that a conservative would never have done. In the central part of her book, she allows the monster to speak for himself, to tell the story from his own perspective. Her choice expresses the liberal attitude to freedom of speech at its most radical: everyone's point of view should be heard. In *Frankenstein*, the monster is not a Thing, a horrible object no one dares to confront; rather, he is fully *subjectivized*. Mary Shelley moves inside his mind and asks what it is like to be labelled, defined, oppressed, excommunicated, even physically distorted, by society. The ultimate criminal is thereby allowed to present himself as the ultimate victim. The monstrous murderer reveals himself to be a deeply hurt and desperate individual, yearning for company and love. There is, however, a clear limit to this procedure. Are we also ready to affirm that Hitler was only an enemy because his story was not heard? Or, on the contrary, is it the case that the more I know about and 'understand' Hitler, the more Hitler is my enemy? The move from the externality of an act to its 'inner meaning', the narrative by means of which the agent interprets and justifies it, is a move towards a deceitful mask. The experience that we have of our lives from within, the story we tell ourselves about ourselves in order to account for what we are doing, is fundamentally a lie. Rather, the truth lies outside, in our actions, in what we do.

The next taboo that we must discard is the all too fast equation of the European emancipatory legacy to cultural imperialism and racism: many on the Left tend to dismiss any mention of 'European values' as the ideological form of Eurocentric colonialism. In spite of Europe's partial responsibility for the situation from which refugees are fleeing, the time has come to drop the Leftist mantra according to which our main task is the critique of Eurocentrism. One evident lesson of the post-9/11 world is that Francis Fukuyama's dream of global liberal democracy has proved illusory. But, nevertheless, at the economic level, capitalism has triumphed worldwide: the developing nations that have endorsed it − China, Vietnam, etc. − are those which are now growing at spectacular rates.

Global capitalism has no problem in accommodating itself to a plurality of local religions, cultures, traditions: indeed, the mask of cultural diversity is sustained by the actual universalism of global capital. And this new global capitalism functions even better if it is politically organized according to the so-called 'Asian values', i.e., in an authoritarian way. So the cruel irony of anti-Eurocentrism is that, on behalf of anti-colonialism, one criticizes the West at the very historical moment when global capitalism no longer needs Western cultural values in order to function smoothly, and is doing quite well with the 'alternative modernity' – the non-democratic form of capitalist modernization – to be found in Asian capitalism. In short, critics of Eurocentrism are rejecting Western cultural values at the very moment when, critically reinterpreted, many of them – egalitarianism, fundamental human rights, the welfare state, to name a few – can serve as a weapon against capitalist globalization. Have we already forgotten, in fact, that the entire idea of Communist emancipation as envisaged by Marx is a thoroughly 'Eurocentric' one?

Another taboo to be jettisoned is the notion that the protection of one's specific way of life is in itself a proto-Fascist or racist category. The idea goes something like this: if we insist on protecting our way of life, we open up the way for the anti-immigrant wave which thrives all around Europe and whose latest sign is the fact that, in the recent Swedish elections, the anti-immigrant Democratic party for the first time overtook the Social Democrats to become the strongest party in the country. However, addressing the concerns of ordinary people about the threats to their specific way of life can be done also from the Leftist standpoint – something of which the Democratic US politician Bernie Sanders is living proof. It needs to be said that the true threat to our common way of life does not come in the shape of refugees but lies in the dynamic of global capitalism. In the US, for example, the economic changes introduced by 'Reaganomics' did more to destroy communal life in small cities – the way ordinary people participated in political events and endeavoured to resolve their local problems collectively – than all the immigrants together! The standard Left-liberal reaction to any mention of 'protecting our way of life' is, of course, an explosion of arrogant moralism: according to this reaction, the moment we give any credence to the 'protection of our way of life' motif we irredeemably compromise ourselves, since all we are doing is proposing a more modest version of what anti-immigrant populists openly advocate. Indeed, is this not the story of recent decades in Europe? Centrist parties reject the open racism of anti-immigrant populists, but they simultaneously profess to 'understand the concerns' of ordinary people and enact a more 'rational' version of the same politics.

And yet another Leftist taboo that needs to be abandoned is that of prohibiting any critique of Islam as a case of 'Islamophobia'. This taboo is a true mirror-image of the anti-immigrant populist demonization of Islam, so we should get rid of the pathological fear of many Western liberal Leftists that they might be guilty of Islamophobia. Recall how Salman Rushdie was denounced for unnecessarily provoking Muslims and thus held responsible (partially, at least) for the *fatwa* condemning him to death – all of a sudden the crux of the problem was not the *fatwa* as such, but the way we might have aroused the ire of the Muslim rulers of Iran . . .[13] The result of such a stance is what one might expect: the more Western liberal

Leftists probe their own guilt, the more they are accused by Muslim fundamentalists of being hypocrites who try to conceal their hatred of Islam. Such a paradigm perfectly reproduces the paradox of the superego: the more you obey what the pseudo-moral agency demands of you, the more guilty you are. It is as if the more you tolerate Islam, the stronger its pressure on you will be. One can be sure that the same holds true for the influx of refugees: the more Western Europe is open to them, the more it will be made to feel guilty that it failed to accept even more of them, that it can never accept enough. Similarly, in accommodating refugees, the more tolerance one displays towards their way of life, the more one will be made to feel guilt for not practising enough tolerance – Muslim children are not served pork in schools, but what if the pork eaten by other children disturbs them; they are allowed to be covered in schools, but what about the half-dressed local girls who disturb them; their religion is tolerated but their religion is not treated with respect by others; etc., etc. The silent premise of the critics of Islamophobia is that Islam somehow resists global capitalism, that it is the privileged obstacle to its unconstrained expansion – consequently, whatever our reservations about it, we should tactically pass over them on behalf of solidarity in the Great Struggle. This premise has to be unequivocally rejected. The political choices provided by Islam can be clearly identified: they reach from Fascist nihilism, which parasitizes on capitalism, up to what Saudi Arabia stands for – can one imagine a country more integrated into global capitalism than Saudi Arabia or one of the Emirates? The most Islam can offer (in its 'moderate' version) is yet another 'alternative modernity', a vision of capitalism without its antagonisms, which cannot but resemble Fascism.

A further, much more subtle, taboo to be left behind is the equation of politicized religion with fanaticism, and the related portrayal of Islamists as pre-modern 'irrational' fanatics. Against such fanaticism, some secularists (like Sam Harris) praise those who practise religion (participate in religious rituals) without believing in it, merely respecting it as part of their culture. It was in fact Islam that both introduced and fully asserted this distinction. While in Western liberal-secular societies, state power protects public freedom and intervenes into the private space (for instance when it suspects child abuse), such 'intrusions into domestic space, the breaching of "private" domains, is disallowed in Islamic law, although conformity in "public" behavior may be much stricter' (37)[14]: 'for the community, what matters is the Muslim subject's social practice – including verbal publication – not her internal thoughts, whatever they may be' (40). Although, as the Qur'an says, 'let him who wills have faith, and him who wills reject it', this 'right to think whatever one wishes does not . . . include the right to express one's religious or moral beliefs publicly with the intention of converting people to a false commitment' (40).

Nevertheless, such non-believing participation in religious ritual can be just as violent as 'sincere' religious fanaticism. An interesting accident took place in New York in June 2015, when gay groups in the city were publicly celebrating the recent federal legalization of gay marriages. Some of their opponents organized counter-demonstrations. Orthodox Jews of the Jewish Political Action Committee hired Mexican labourers to dress up as Jews and do the protesting for them, bearing signs that read things like 'Judaism prohibits homosexuality' and 'God Created Adam and Eve NOT Adam and Steve'. Heshie Freed, the group's representative, justified this act by claiming the Mexicans were filling in for the Jews to protect them from moral corruption: 'The rabbis said that the yeshiva boys shouldn't come out for this because of what they would see at the parade.' As an acerbic critic commented, the Jewish boys were probably 'down in the street rockin' out with their cocks out' in the gay parade.[15] A wonderful new and unexpected vision of inter-passivity – I hire others to protest for me while I participate in the very thing I protest against through the other. This is a nice example of how even a non-believer can enjoy the practical consequences of belief. One might not, for instance, believe in God, but nonetheless believe that God gave your people the land they claim.

In a speech in mid-2015, Israel's Deputy Foreign Minister Tzipi Hotovely reportedly

> told new members of the foreign ministry staff . . . that Israel should no longer speak in veiled terms about possessing the land because God gave it to the Jews. [Hotovely] quoted a medieval Jewish rabbi, Rashi, who wrote about the creation of the world. In that account, the rabbi suggested: 'For if the nations of the world

should say to Israel, "You are robbers, for you conquered by force the lands of the seven nations [of Canaan]," they will reply, "The entire earth belongs to the Holy One, blessed be He; He created it (this we learn from the story of the Creation) and gave it to whomever He deemed proper when He wished. He gave it to them, and when He wished, He took it away from them and gave it to us.' According to Hotovely, Israel should be following the same policy today because it is time to 'tell the world we're right – and smart.'[16]

With such enlightened friends of the West, who needs fundamentalist enemies? If such a direct legitimization of one's claim to land by reference to God's will is not religious fundamentalism, then we should wonder if this term has any meaning at all . . . However, we should also note here the openly cynical twist introduced by the concluding predicate: 'we're right – and smart': we're right in claiming God gave us this land, and 'smart' in using this religious justification although we know it's nonsense. But even if we take seriously the claim that the land of Israel was given to the Jews by God, how did this come about? The Old Testament describes this gift in terms of ethnic cleansing. After their liberation from slavery in Egypt, the Israelites arrived on the edge of the Promised Land, where God commanded them to obliterate the people then occupying these regions (the Canaanites); the Israelites, indeed, were to 'not leave alive anything that breathes' (Deuteronomy 20:16). The Book of Joshua records how the Israelites carried out this command: 'they devoted the city to the LORD and destroyed with the sword every living thing in it – men and women, young and old, cattle, sheep and donkeys' (Joshua 6:21). Several chapters later, we read that Joshua, the Israelite leader, 'left no survivors. He totally destroyed all who breathed, just as the LORD, the God of Israel, had commanded' (10:40). The text mentions city after city in which Joshua, at God's command, puts everyone to the sword, totally annihilating the inhabitants and leaving no survivors (10:28, 30, 33, 37, 39, 40; 11:8). Should we condemn Judaism for these deeds? No, of course not. We find similar passages in all classic religious texts, Buddhist ones included.[17] What we should do, however, is unambiguously reject the direct use of these passages as a legitimization of contemporary politics. Moreover, we should ignore them not only because they are not essential to the immanent content of the religion in question, but also because their oppressive use is conditioned by specific historical circumstances.

Unfortunately, though, the Israeli government is being sucked deeper and deeper into this mire. In a speech to the World Zionist Congress in Jerusalem on 21 October 2015, Prime Minister Binyamin Netanyahu suggested that Hitler had wanted only to expel Jews from Germany, not to exterminate them; and that, rather, it was Haj Amin al-Husseini, the Palestinian grand mufti of Jerusalem, who somehow persuaded Hitler to kill the Jews instead. Netanyahu purported to describe an exchange between the two men in November 1941, in which al-Husseini told Hitler that if he expelled the Jews from Europe, 'they'll all come here [to Palestine]'. According to Netanyahu, Hitler then asked: 'What should I do with them?', to which the mufti replied: 'Burn them.' Many of Israel's top Holocaust researchers immediately problematized these statements, pointing out that the exchange between al-Husseini and Hitler cannot be verified, and that the mass killings of European Jews by SS mobile killing units was already well under way by the time the two men met. Reacting to Netanyahu's comments, the opposition leader Isaac Herzog wrote: 'This is a dangerous historical distortion and I demand Netanyahu correct it immediately as it minimizes the Holocaust, Nazism and . . . Hitler's part in our people's terrible disaster.' He added that Netanyahu's remarks played into the hands of Holocaust deniers. The Zionist Union MP Itzik Shmuli called on Netanyahu to apologize to Holocaust victims: 'This is a great shame, a prime minister of the Jewish state at the service of Holocaust-deniers – this is a first.' Denouncing Netanyahu's comments, Saeb Erekat, the chief Palestinian peace negotiator, wrote: 'It is a sad day in history when the leader of the Israeli government hates his neighbor so much so that he is willing to absolve the most notorious war criminal in history, Adolf Hitler, of the murder of 6 million Jews during the Holocaust.' A spokesman for Angela Merkel also rejected Netanyahu's framing: 'All Germans know the history of the murderous race mania of the Nazis that led to the break with civilization that was the Holocaust. I see no reason to change our view of history in any way. We know that responsibility for this crime against humanity is German and very much our own.'[18] We should be under no illusions about the meaning of statements like those of Netanyahu: they are a clear sign of the regression of our public sphere. Accusations and ideas that were until now confined to the obscure underworld of racist obscenity are now gaining a foothold in official discourse.

There is nonetheless one good thing about the intolerance of religious fundamentalisms: that they cannot tolerate *each other*. That is to say, there is no danger of any 'united front' of Christian and Muslim fundamentalists in Europe (if one disregards minor collaborations like their shared efforts to criminalize 'disrespectful' writing about religion as hate speech).

The European Muslim community (which reaches well beyond fundamentalists), meanwhile, confronts a paradoxical predicament. Although there are many Christian and Muslim liberals who show great tolerance for each other, the only political force that does not reduce Muslims to second-class citizens and which allows them the space to deploy their religious identity are the 'godless' atheist liberals. Those who are closest to their social-religious practice, their Christian mirror-image, are by contrast their greatest political enemies. The paradox is that their only true allies are those who, out of solidarity with freedom of expression, reprinted the Muhammad caricatures.

The Obscene Underside
of Religions

Any critical examination of the dark potential of Islam should undoubtedly embrace Judaism and Christianity as well. Much work has already been done here: the obscene underside of the Catholic universe is a topic that is over-analysed in our societies, as are the parallels between Jewish, Christian and Muslim fundamentalisms. Let's recall events in the Yorkshire town of Rotherham in England, where, between 1997 and 2013, at least 1,400 children were subjected to brutal sexual exploitation. Children as young as 11 were raped by multiple perpetrators, abducted, trafficked to other cities, beaten and intimidated, 'doused in petrol and threatened with being set alight, threatened with guns, made to witness brutally violent rapes and threatened they would be next if they told anyone, as the official report put it'.[19] Before a comprehensive inquiry was published in 2014, there had been three inquiries in the early to mid-2000s which had led to nothing: the inquiry team noted fears among council staff of being labelled 'racist' if they pursued the matter. The perpetrators were almost exclusively members of Pakistani gangs, and their victims (referred to by the perpetrators as 'white trash') white schoolgirls.

Reactions were predictable.[20] Exhibiting Political Correctness at its worst, many on the Left resorted to all possible strategies of blurring the contours, mostly through generalizations. Perpetrators were designated vaguely as 'Asians', while claims were made that the abuse was not about ethnicity and religion but about domination of man over woman; and anyway, who are we, with our Church paedophilia and sexual abuse scandals – that of the media personality Jimmy Saville being a case in point – to adopt the moral high ground over a victimized minority? Can one imagine a response that would more effectively open up the field to UKIP and other anti-immigrant populists who exploit the worries of ordinary people? Such apparent anti-racism is effectively a barely covert racism, condescendingly treating Pakistanis as morally inferior beings who should not be held to our standards.

In order to break out of this deadlock of Leftist liberalism and its inability seriously to confront racial and religious violence, one should begin with the parallel between the Rotherham events and the widespread paedophilia within the Catholic Church. In both cases, we are dealing with organized – ritualized even – collective activity. In the case of Rotherham, another parallel may be even more pertinent. One of the terrifying effects of the non-contemporaneity of different levels of social life – behaviour that somehow seems out of sync with the age in which we live – is the rise of the violence against women. By this I mean not just random violence, but systematic violence: violence that is specific to a certain social context, follows a pattern, and transmits a clear message. While we were right to be terrified and appalled by the gang rapes in India, the worldwide echo of these cases (they were reported in the main media of all Western countries) is nonetheless suspicious: as Arundhati Roy has pointed out, these rapes triggered such a unanimous outburst of moral reaction also because the rapists were poor, from the lower strata. So, perhaps, we need to widen our frame of reference and include other similar phenomena. The serial killings of women in Ciudad Juárez at the border with Texas are not just private pathologies, but, again, a ritualized activity, part of the subculture of local gangs (first gang rape, then torture to death, including the cutting off of nipples with scissors and other horrific acts), which is directed at single young women working in factories: a clear case, it would seem, of a macho reaction to a new class of independent working women.[21]

Even more unexpected than the Ciudad Juárez killings (from our racist perspective, one somehow expects brutal Mexican machos to act in this way) are the recent serial rapes and murders of aboriginal women in Western Canada, close to reservations around Vancouver, which belie Canada's claim to be the model of a tolerant welfare state: a group of white men abduct, rape and kill a woman, and then deposit the mutilated body just within the reservation territory, thereby putting it legally under the jurisdiction of the tribal police, who are totally unprepared to deal with such cases. When Canadian authorities are contacted, as a rule they limit their investigation to the native community, in order to present the crime as a case of local family violence due to drugs and alcohol. In these

cases, social dislocation – the result, often, of rapid indus-
trialization and modernization – provokes a brutal
reaction in males, who experience such development as
a threat. And the crucial feature in all these cases is that
these acts of criminal violence are not spontaneous
outbursts of raw brutal energy that breaks the chains of
civilized customs, but something learned, externally
imposed, ritualized: part of the collective symbolic substance of a community. What is repressed for the
'innocent' public gaze is not the cruel brutality of the act,
but precisely its 'cultural', ritualistic character of a symbolic custom.[22]

The same perverted social-ritual logic is at work in the
cases of paedophilia that constantly shatter the Catholic
Church. When Church representatives insist that these
cases, deplorable as they are, are the Church's internal
problem – and consequently display great reluctance to
collaborate with police in their investigation – they are, in
a way, right. The paedophilia of Catholic priests is not
something that concerns only the persons who, because
of accidental reasons of a private history that has no relation to the Church as an institution, happen to choose the
profession of a priest. This abuse is a phenomenon that
concerns the Catholic Church as such, because it is
inscribed into its very functioning as a socio-symbolic
institution. In this way, it does not concern only the 'private' unconscious of individuals but also the 'unconscious'
of the institution of the Catholic Church itself. This abuse
is not something that happens because the institution has
to accommodate itself to the pathological realities of

libidinal life in order to survive, but something that the institution itself needs in order to reproduce itself. One can well imagine a non-paedophiliac priest who, after years of service, gets involved in paedophilia because the very logic of the institution seduces him into it. Such an 'institutional unconscious' designates the obscene disavowed underside that sustains the public institution. (In the army, this underside consists of obscene sexualized rituals such as hazing, which sustain group solidarity.) In other words, it is not simply that, for conformist reasons, the Church tries to hush up its paedophilic scandals; rather, in defending itself, the Church is defending its innermost obscene secret. What this means is that identifying oneself with this secret side is a key constituent of the very identity of a Catholic priest. If a priest seriously – not just rhetorically – denounces these scandals, he thereby excludes himself from the ecclesiastic community, he is no longer 'one of us'. (In exactly the same way, a citizen of a town in the South of the US in the 1920s, if he denounced Ku Klux Klan to the police, excluded himself from his community, i.e. betrayed its fundamental solidarity.)

We should approach the Rotherham events in exactly the same way. Here, we are dealing with the 'political unconscious' of the Pakistani Muslim youth. Not with chaotic violence but with a ritualized violence that has precise ideological contours: a group of (mostly) young people which experiences itself as marginalized and subordinated, exacting revenge on vulnerable, lower-class girls from the predominant group. In this context, it is

fully legitimate to ask whether there are religious and cultural features of their community that open up the
possibility of such brutality against women. Without
blaming Islam (which is no more misogynistic than Christianity), one can observe that violence against women
resonates with the subordination of women and their
exclusion from public life in many Muslim countries and
communities; it might also be added that, among many
groups and movements designated as fundamentalist, the
strict imposition of a hierarchic sexual difference is at the
very top of their agenda.

So, simply, we should apply the same criteria on both
sides, without fear of admitting that, while our Christian
fundamentalists are more marginalized than those of the
Muslim world (who takes Christian fundamentalists really
seriously?), our liberal-secular critique of fundamentalism
is also stained by falsity. Let us take an example from liberal society at its best, a recent scandalous legal case in
Canada. In March 2015, Bradley Barton from Ontario was
found not guilty of first-degree murder following the
death in 2011 of Cindy Gladue, an indigenous 36-year-old
sex worker who bled to death at the Yellowhead Inn in
Edmonton, having sustained an 11-centimetre wound on
her vaginal wall. The prosecution claimed that the wound
was caused by a sharp object or by Barton's excessive
thrusting with his hand, while the defence argued that
Barton accidentally caused Gladue's death during rough
but consensual sex (but then again, how could she give
consent when her blood-alcohol level was, as shown in
the trial, extremely high?). Barton admitted to his actions,

but he said he didn't mean them. Furthermore, a laptop found with Barton's belongings was not admitted as evidence, although it had a search history of pornography depicting torture. This case doesn't just run counter to our basic ethical intuitions (a man brutally murders a woman during sexual activity but he walks free because 'he didn't mean it'?). The most disturbing aspect is that, acceding to the demands of the defence, the judge allowed Gladue's preserved pelvis to be admitted as evidence: brought into court, the lower part of her torso was displayed for the jurors (incidentally, this is the first time a portion of a body has been presented at a trial in Canada). Why would photographs of the wound not be enough? Does such a display not rely on the long tradition of treating indigenous peoples' bodies as specimens? Could we even imagine the opposite case, an upper-class white woman's torso displayed when the accused is a black or indigenous man?[23]

Divine Violence

The alternatives of pragmatic secular politics and religious fundamentalism don't cover the entire field of politico-religious options. Leaving aside the (deplorable near-absence of) radical emancipatory politics in our world today, there is an ominous phenomenon that, perhaps, fits what Walter Benjamin called 'divine violence'. In August 2014, protests exploded in Ferguson, a suburb of St Louis, after a policeman shot dead an unarmed black teenager suspected of robbery: for days afterwards, police tried to disperse the protesters, mostly African Americans. Although the details of the incident are murky, the poor black majority of the town took the killing as yet more proof of a systemic police violence against them. In US slums and ghettos, it seems that increasingly the police effectively function as a force of occupation, something akin to Israeli patrols entering the Palestinian territories on the West Bank: media were surprised to discover that the guns they use are more and more likely to be US army-issue guns. Even when police units try just to impose order, distribute humanitarian help or organize medical measures, their modus operandi is like that of a force trying to control a foreign population. Are the apparently 'irrational' violent demonstrations such as that in Ferguson, with no concrete programmatic demands but rather motivated and sustained by just a vague call for justice, not today's exemplary cases of divine violence? They are not part of a long-term strategy, i.e., as Benjamin put it, they are means without ends. Benjamin argues against

the stubborn prevailing habit of conceiving those just ends as ends of a possible law, that is, not only as generally valid (which follows analytically from the nature of justice), but also as capable of generalization, which, as could be shown, contradicts the nature of justice. For ends that for one situation are just, universally acceptable, and valid, are so for no other situation, no matter how similar it may be in other respects. The non-mediate function of violence at issue here is illustrated by everyday experience. As regards man, he is impelled by anger, for example, to the most visible outbursts of a violence that is not related as a means to a preconceived end. It is not a means but a manifestation.[24]

One has to note the paradox of this formula: for our common sense, general validity should be 'stronger' than (the process of) generalization, since it is its result, the outcome of successful generalization – so how can something be general(ly valid) and yet not generalizable (or, rather, universally valid and not universalizable)? An example (referred to by Kant) may clarify this distinction. 'Don't steal!' is a universal moral injunction (it tolerates no exceptions, it tells you never to steal), but it cannot be universalized since its (universal) validity is confined to

36

the domain of (private) property: it is meaningless to apply it to domains in which things are not owned by anyone. Similarly, the mistake of the standard notion of (social) violence is to limit it to its use as a means: in what circumstances it may be legitimate to resort to violence, and so on. Although in this way we can elaborate universal(ly valid) rules (like 'never resort to violence when you can achieve your goal through non-violent means'), such an approach is not universalizable, since it doesn't cover the cases in which violence 'is not related as a means to a preconceived end'. As Le Gaufey points out,[25] therein resides the difference between Carl Schmitt and Benjamin. Schmitt remains constrained by the idea that legitimate violence has to be a means to an end, which is why the most radical expression of violence he can imagine is that of mythic violence, violence that serves the end of grounding the rule of law (even when it violates the existing legal order); Benjamin's 'divine violence' is rather, as he put it, a case of a means without an end.

Does not the same hold not only for other protests which followed Ferguson, like the Baltimore riots in April 2015, but also for the French suburban riots of autumn 2005, when we saw thousands of cars burning and a major outburst of public violence? In these protests, what strikes the eye is the total absence of any positive utopian prospect among the protesters: if May '68 was a revolt with a utopian vision, the 2005 revolts in France were outbursts with no pretensions to vision. If the oft-repeated commonplace that we live in a post-ideological era has any sense, it is here. There were no particular demands made by the protesters in the Paris suburbs. There was only an insistence on *recognition*, based on a vague, non-articulated, *ressentiment*. Most of those interviewed after the event talked about how unacceptable it was that the then interior minister, Nicolas Sarkozy, had called them 'scum'. In a weird self-referential short-circuit, they were (also) protesting against the very reaction (by Sarkozy) that their protests inspired. Populist reason here encounters its irrational limit: what we have is a zero-level protest, a violent act of protest that demands nothing. There was an irony in watching the sociologists, intellectuals and commentators trying to understand and help. Desperately they tried to translate these events into the meaning they superimposed on them: 'We must do something about the integration of immigrants, about their welfare, their job opportunities,' they proclaimed, and in the process obfuscated the key enigma the riots presented . . .

We should remember that the Paris protesters, although underprivileged and effectively excluded from mainstream French society, were in no way living on the edge of starvation. Nor had they been reduced to the level of bare survival. People in much more terrible material straits, let alone conditions of physical and ideological oppression, have been able to organize themselves into political agents with fuzzy or even clear agendas. The fact that there was *no* programme in the burning Paris suburbs is thus itself a fact to be interpreted. It tells us a great deal about our ideologico-political situation. What kind of universe is it that we inhabit, which celebrates itself as a society of choice but in which the only available alternative to the enforced democratic consensus is a blind acting out? The sad fact that an opposition to the system cannot present itself as a realistic alternative, or at least articulate a meaningful utopian project, but can only take the shape of a meaningless outburst, is a grave indictment of our predicament. What does our celebrated freedom of choice serve, when the only choice is between playing by the rules and (self-)destructive violence? The protesters' violence was almost exclusively directed against their own. The cars burned and the schools torched were not those of richer neighbourhoods; they were part of the hard-won acquisitions of the very social strata from which the protesters originated.

What, then, needs to be resisted when faced with the shocking reports and images of the burning Paris suburbs and other similar incidents is what I call the hermeneutic temptation: the search for some deeper meaning or message hidden in these outbursts. What is most difficult to accept is precisely the riots' meaninglessness: more than a form of protest, they are what Lacan called a *passage à l'acte* – an impulsive movement into action which cannot be translated into speech or thought, and which carries with it an intolerable weight of frustration. This bears witness not only to the impotence of the perpetrators, but, even more, to the lack of what Fredric Jameson has called 'cognitive mapping', an inability to locate the experience of their situation within a meaningful whole. It is against this background that one should read the surprising lines about divine violence from Werner Kraft's diary. Writing on 20 May 1934, Kraft reports on Benjamin's reflection on his own 'Critique of Violence', written over a decade previously:

A just right [*gerechtes Recht*] is what serves the oppressed in class struggle. – Class struggle is the center of all philosophical questions, including the highest ones. – What he earlier called divine ('ruling') violence was an empty spot, a liminal notion, a regulative idea. Now he knows that it is class struggle. – Violence which is justified has nothing to do with a sanction, it doesn't add anything to the thing, it is without a sensible image like for example the 'crown' of a king, etc. One can kill, when one does it in this way, like one kills an ox. The 'just war' at the end of the article on violence: class struggle.[26]

The immediate counter-argument is this: are such violent demonstrations not often unjust; do they not hurt the innocent? If we are to avoid the overstretched Politically Correct explanations, according to which the victims of divine violence should humbly and passively take what comes to them on account of their generic historical responsibility, the only solution is to simply accept the fact that divine violence *is* brutally unjust: it is often something terrifying, not a sublime intervention of divine goodness and justice. A Left-liberal friend from the University of Chicago told me of a distressing experience: when his son reached high-school age, he enrolled him into a school north of the campus, close to a black ghetto, with a majority of black kids. Not long after, his son was returning home with bruises or broken teeth. So what should he have done? Put his son into another school with a white majority or keep him in this first school? The point is that this dilemma is wrong: it cannot be solved at such a level, since the very gap between private interest (safety of the son) and global justice bears witness to a situation which has to be overcome. The same holds for Palestinians stabbing Israelis with knives, maybe yet another case of divine violence.

The sad conclusion that imposes itself here is a double one. First, there is nothing noble or sublime about what Benjamin calls divine violence – it is 'divine' precisely on account of its excessively destructive character. Second, we have to abandon the idea that there is something emancipatory in extreme experiences, that they enable us to open our eyes to the ultimate truth of a situation. There is a memorable passage in Ruth Klüger's *Still Alive: A Holocaust Girlhood Remembered*, in which she describes a conversation with some advanced PhD candidates in Germany:

> One reports how in Jerusalem he made the acquaintance of an old Hungarian Jew who was a survivor of Auschwitz, and yet this man cursed the Arabs and held them all in contempt. How can someone who comes from Auschwitz talk like that? the German asks. I get into the act and argue, perhaps more hotly than need be. What did he expect? Auschwitz was no instructional institution . . . You learned nothing there, and least of all humanity and tolerance. Absolutely nothing good came out of the concentration camps, I hear myself saying,

with my voice rising, and he expects catharsis, purgation, the sort of thing you go to the theatre for? They were the most useless, pointless establishments imaginable.[27]

This, perhaps, is the most depressing lesson of horror and suffering: there is nothing to be learned from it. The only way out of the vicious circle of this depression is to change the terrain towards concrete social and economic analysis.

The Political Economy of Refugees

A good way to begin this analysis is to focus on what one cannot but call the 'political economy of refugees', in order to develop a clear awareness of what and who is causing such mass movements of people. Here, the first step is of course to locate the ultimate cause in the dynamics of global capitalism, as well as in the process of Western military intervention. In short, this ongoing disorder is the true face of the New World Order. Left to themselves, Africans will not succeed in changing their societies. Why not? Because we, Western Europeans, are preventing them from doing so. It was European intervention in Libya that threw the country into chaos. It was the US attack on Iraq that created the conditions for the rise of ISIS. The ongoing civil war in the Central African Republic between the Christian south and the Muslim north is not just an explosion of ethnic hatred. Rather, this explosion was triggered by the discovery of oil in the north of the country: France (linked to Muslims) and China (linked to Christians) are fighting for the control of oil resources through their proxies.

Blame for the food crisis in many countries in the global south cannot be put on the usual suspects like corruption, inefficiency and state interventionism. The crisis stems directly from the globalization of agriculture, as none other than Bill Clinton made clear in his comments on the global food crisis at a UN gathering marking World Food Day (as reported on 23 October 2008 under the indicative headline ' "We Blew It" On Global Food'[28]). The gist of Clinton's speech was that today's global food crisis shows how 'we all blew it, including me when I was president', by treating food crops as commodities instead of as a vital right of the world's poor. In his speech, Clinton was very clear in putting blame not on individual states or governments, but on long-term global Western policy imposed by the US and the European Union and enacted for decades by the World Bank, the International Monetary Fund and others international institutions. This policy pressured African and Asian countries into jettisoning government subsidies for fertilizer, improved seed and other farm inputs, thereby opening up the way for the best land to be used for export crops and in this way ruining the countries' food self-sufficiency. The result of such 'structural adjustments' was the integration of local agriculture into the global economy: while crops were exported, farmers thrown off their land were pushed into slums, available as a workforce for outsourced sweatshops. As a result, these countries had to rely more and more on imported food. In this way, they are kept in post-colonial dependence, and are more and more vulnerable to market fluctuations: the skyrocketing of grain prices (also caused by the use of crops for biofuels) in recent years has caused starvation in countries from Haiti to Ethiopia. If we are to deal with these problems properly, we will have to invent new forms of large-scale collective action: neither the standard state intervention nor the local self-organizations (so much praised by postmodern Leftists) can do the job. If we cannot solve this problem, we should seriously entertain the possibility that we are approaching a new era of apartheid: one in which secluded parts of the world with an abundance of food and energy are separated from a chaotic outside plagued by widespread turbulence, starvation and permanent war. What should people in today's Haiti and other regions hit by food shortages do? Do they not have the full right to violently rebel? Or indeed to become refugees . . .

In spite of all the criticism of economic neo-colonialism, many are still not fully aware of the devastating effects of the global market on many local economies, depriving them of their elementary self-sufficiency. Suffice it to recall the case of Mexico, a food-importer with a ruined local agriculture exporting millions of its inhabitants to the US. But the clearest case of our guilt is today's Congo, which is once again emerging as the African 'heart of darkness'.

The cover story of *Time* magazine on 5 June 2006 was headlined 'The Deadliest War in the World' – a detailed documentation of how around four million people had died in Congo as the result of political violence over the previous decade. But none of the usual humanitarian uproar followed, as if some kind of filtering mechanism had blocked this news from achieving its full impact. To put it cynically, *Time* had picked the wrong victim in the struggle for hegemony in suffering. It should have stuck to the list of usual suspects: Muslim women and their plight, oppression in Tibet, and so on. (Today, the same state of things – continuous violence in a failed state – goes on in Congo, as well as many other African countries from the Central African Republic to Libya.) Why this extraordinary lack of response to reports of such massive loss of life?

Back in 2001, a UN investigation into the illegal exploitation of natural resources in Congo found that the conflict in the country is mainly about access to, control of, and trade in five key mineral resources: coltan, diamonds, copper, cobalt and gold. Beneath the façade of ethnic warfare, we thus discern the workings of global capitalism. Congo no longer exists as a united state; it is a multiplicity of territories ruled by local warlords controlling their patch of land with armies that, as a rule, include drugged children. Each of these warlords has business links to a foreign company or corporation exploiting the mostly mining wealth in the region. The irony is that many of these minerals are used in high-tech products such as laptops and cell phones.

So forget about the savage behaviour of the local population: just remove the foreign high-tech companies from the equation and the whole narrative of ethnic warfare fuelled by old passions falls apart. This is where we should begin if we really want to help stop the flow of refugees from African countries. The first thing is to recall that most refugees come from 'failed states', states where public authority is more or less inoperative, at least in large parts of the countries in question (Syria, Lebanon, Iraq,

Libya, Somalia, Congo, and so on). In all these instances, this disintegration of state power is not purely a local phenomenon but the result of international economics and politics; in some cases, such as in Libya and Iraq, it is even a direct outcome of Western intervention. It is clear that this rise of 'failed states' in the late twentieth and twenty-first centuries is not an unintended misfortune; rather, it is one of the ways in which the great powers practise their economic colonialism. One should also note that the origins of the Middle Eastern 'failed states' are to be found in the arbitrary borders drawn after the First World War by the UK and France, which thereby created a series of 'artificial' states. In uniting Sunnis in Syria and Iraq, ISIS is ultimately bringing together what was torn apart by the colonial masters. In a gloomy prophecy made before his death, Colonel Gaddafi said:

> Now listen you, people of NATO. You're bombing a wall which stood in the way of African migration to Europe, and in the way of Al-Qaeda terrorists. This wall was Libya. You're breaking it. You're idiots, and you will burn in Hell for thousands of migrants from Africa.[29]

Was he not stating the obvious? The Russian story – which basically elaborates Gaddafi's point – has its moment of truth, in spite of the obvious taste of *pasta putinesca*:

> 'That the refugee crisis is an outcome of US–European policies is clear to the naked eye,' says Boris Dolgov (a member of the Russian Academy of Sciences and the

Institute of Oriental Studies in Moscow). 'The destruction of Iraq, the destruction of Libya and attempts to
topple Bashar Assad in Syria with the hands of Islamic
radicals – that's what EU and US policies are all about,
and the hundreds of thousands of refugees are a result
of that policy.' 'It's a very serious and multi-faceted
problem,' Irina Zvyagelskaya (Vice President of the
International Center for Strategic and Political Studies,
Moscow) told the Russian News Agency TASS. 'The
civil war in Syria and tensions in Iraq and Libya keep
fueling the flow of migrants, but that is not the only
cause. I agree with those who see the current events as a
trend towards another mass resettlement of peoples,
which leave the weaker countries with ineffective economies. There are systemic problems that cause people to
abandon their homes and take to the road. And the liberal European legislation allows many of them to not
only stay in Europe, but also to live there on social
benefits without seeking employment.' 'These people are exhausted, angry and humiliated. They have no
idea of European values, lifestyles and traditions, multiculturalism or tolerance. They will never agree to abide
by European laws,' says the Russian writer and dramatist
Yevgeny Grishkovets in his blog. 'They will never feel
grateful to the people whose countries they have managed to get into with such problems, because the very
same states first turned their own home countries into a
bloodbath ... Angela Merkel vows modern German
society and Europe are prepared for problems ... That's
a lie and nonsense!'[30]

It is by and large true that the refugees 'will never feel grateful to the people whose countries they have managed to get into': indeed, they perceive Europe as responsible for their predicament. However, while there is some general truth in all this, one should not jump from this generality to the empirical fact of refugees flowing into Europe and simply accept our full responsibility for them. First, we should remember that Germany and France were resolutely against the 2003 war on Iraq. Second, the regime of Saddam Hussein had, prior to its overthrow, pursued its own aggressive politics – instanced particularly in its attack on Iran in 1980, in which it was silently supported by the US. But what should surprise us is how our media present the current refugee crisis. It is more or less as if beyond Greece there is a kind of black hole spewing out refugees, a black hole of war and devastation, and on the Anatolian coast there exists some kind of loophole through which refugee particles are allowed to escape onto Greek islands. But beyond Greece there is a well-defined political landscape. First, there is Turkey itself, playing a well-planned political game (officially fighting ISIS but effectively bombing Kurds who are really fighting ISIS); then there is the high class division in the Arab world itself (the ultra-rich Saudi Arabia, Kuwait, Qatar, the UAE, all accepting practically no refugees); then there is Iraq itself, with tens of billions in oil money reserves, and so on. How, out of all this mess, does the flow of refugees emerge?

What we do know is that there is a complex economy of refugee transportation (an industry worth billions of dollars[31]); so who is financing it, streamlining it? Where are the European intelligence services to explore this dark netherworld? The fact that refugees are in a desperate situation in no way excludes the possibility that their flow is part of a well-planned project.

One cannot but note the fact that some less well-off Middle East countries (Turkey, Egypt, Iran, etc.) are much more open to the refugees than the really wealthy ones (Saudi Arabia, Kuwait, the UAE, Qatar and so on). Saudi Arabia and the Emirates have taken almost no refugees, although they are neighbours of the area of crisis, as well as rich and culturally much closer to the refugees (who are mostly Muslims) than Europe. In fact, Saudi Arabia even repatriated some Muslim refugees back to Somalia[32] – all it did was to contribute US$280 million in support of the education of refugees. Is this because Saudi Arabia is a fundamentalist theocracy that is not able to tolerate foreign intruders? Yes, but one should also bear in mind that this same Saudi Arabia is economically fully integrated into the West: from the economic standpoint, are Saudi Arabia and the Emirates not pure outposts of Western capital, states that depend totally on their oil revenues for their wealth and standing in the world? The international community should put full pressure on Saudi Arabia (and Kuwait, Qatar and so on) to do their duty in accepting a large contingent of the refugees – especially since, by way of supporting the anti-Assad rebels, Saudi Arabia is in large part responsible for the situation in Syria.[33]

Another feature shared by these rich countries is the

rise of a new slavery. While capitalism legitimizes itself as the economic system that implies and furthers personal freedoms (as a condition of market exchange), its own dynamics have brought about a renaissance of slavery. Although slavery became almost extinct at the end of the Middle Ages, it exploded again in the European colonies from early modernity until the American Civil War. And one can risk the hypothesis that today, with the new epoch of global capitalism, a new era of slavery is also arising. While there is no longer a direct legal status of enslaved persons, slavery has acquired a multitude of new forms: millions of immigrant workers in the Saudi peninsula who are deprived of elementary civil rights and freedoms; the total control over millions of workers in Asian sweat-shops often directly organized as concentration camps; the massive use of forced labour in the exploitation of natural resources in many central African states (Congo and so on). But, in fact, we don't have to look so far as these countries. On 1 December 2013, a Chinese-owned clothing factory in an industrial zone in the Italian town of Prato, 10 kilometres from the centre of Florence, burned down, killing seven workers who were trapped inside. Riberto Pistonina, a local trade unionist, com-mented: 'No one can say they are surprised at this because everyone has known for years that, in the area between Florence and Prato, hundreds if not thousands of people are living and working in conditions of near-slavery.' Prato has around 15,000 Chinese people legally registered in a total population of under 200,000, with more than

4,000 Chinese-owned businesses. But thousands more Chinese immigrants are believed to be living in the city illegally, working up to 16 hours a day for a network of wholesalers and workshops turning out cheap clothing.

So we cannot permit ourselves the luxury of looking at the miserable life of new slaves far away in the suburbs of Shanghai (or Dubai and Qatar) and hypocritically criticize the countries that house them. Slavery can be right here, within our house. We just don't see it – or, rather, we pretend not to see it. This new apartheid, this systematic explosion of the number of different forms of *de facto* slavery, is not a deplorable accident but a structural necessity of today's global capitalism. This is perhaps the reason why refugees don't want to enter Saudi Arabia. But, in fact, are not the refugees entering Europe also offering themselves as a cheap precarious workforce, in many cases at the expense of local workers, many of whom react to this threat by joining anti-immigrant populists? For many of the refugees, this rejection by the local poor will be their dream realized.

From the Culture Wars to Class Struggle . . . and Back

For the refugees are not just escaping from their war-torn homelands. They are also possessed by a certain dream. We see again and again on our screens refugees in southern Italy who make it clear that they don't want to stay there: they mostly want to live in Scandinavian countries. And what about the thousands in camps around the channel port of Calais who are not satisfied with France but are ready to risk their lives to enter the United Kingdom? One can observe here the paradox of utopia: precisely when people find themselves in poverty, distress and danger, and one would expect that they would be satisfied by a minimum of safety and well-being, the absolute utopia explodes. But the hard lesson for the refugees is that 'there is no Norway', even in Norway. They will have to learn to censor their dreams: instead of chasing them in reality, they should focus on changing reality.

The refugees take seriously the principle, proclaimed by the EU, of the 'freedom of movement for all' within Europe. But, again, one has to be specific here. There is a concept of 'freedom of movement' in the sense of freedom to travel, and a more radical idea of a 'freedom of movement' that conveys the right to settle in whatever country I want. The axiom that sustains the refugees in

Calais is not just the freedom to travel but something like 'everyone has the right to settle in any other part of the world, and the country they move in to has to provide for them.' The European Union guarantees (sort of, more or less) this right for the citizens of its members – that, among other things, is what the EU is about – and to demand the immediate globalization of this right equals the demand to expand the EU's idea to the entire world. The actualization of this freedom presupposes nothing less than a radical socio-economic revolution – but why?

In our global world, commodities circulate freely, but not people: to reiterate, new forms of apartheid are emerging. The topic of porous walls, of the threat of being inundated by foreigners, is strictly immanent to global capitalism: it is an index of what is false about capitalist globalization. It is as if the refugees want to extend free global circulation from commodities to people. From the Marxist standpoint, the 'freedom of movement' has to be related to the need of capital for a 'free' labour force (millions torn out of their communal life forms so that they can be employed in sweatshops, as is happening today in China or Mexico), as well as to the truly universal freedom of capital to move around the globe. The way the universe of capital relates to the freedom of movement of individuals is thus inherently contradictory: it needs 'free' individuals as cheap labour forces, but it simultaneously needs to control their movement since it cannot afford the same freedoms and rights for all people.

Since one has to start the struggle somewhere, does this mean that the demand for a radical freedom of movement can be, precisely insofar as it cannot be met within the existing world order, a good place to begin? The problem is that the dream of the refugees who want to reach Norway is an exemplary case of ideological fantasy, of a fantasy-formation which obfuscates immanent antagonisms – a fantasy which precisely obliterates *objet petit a* (Lacan's name for the object-cause of desire) as the inherent obstacle that constitutes what it appears to block access to. In short, the refugees want to have their cake and eat it. They basically expect to get the best of the Western welfare state while retaining their specific way of life, which is in some of its key features incompatible with the ideological foundations of the Western welfare state. Germany likes to emphasize the need to integrate the refugees culturally and socially; however – another taboo to be broken – how many of them really want to be integrated? What if the obstacle to integration is not only Western racism? One should move beyond the cliché of refugees as proletarians with 'nothing to lose but their chains' invading bourgeois Europe. There is a class division in Europe as well as in the Middle East, and the key question is: how do these different class dynamics interact?

Let's begin with the US. In his book on the rise of Christian fundamentalism in Kansas, Thomas Frank[34] aptly described the paradox of today's US populist conservatism, whose basic premise is the gap between economic interests and 'moral' questions. That is to say, the opposition of economic classes (poor farmers, blue-collar workers versus lawyers, bankers, large companies) is transposed/coded into an opposition of honest hard-working Christian true Americans versus decadent liberals who drink *lattes* and drive foreign cars, advocate abortion and homosexuality, mock patriotic sacrifice and the 'provincial' simple way of life of the said 'true Americans', and so on. In populist conservatism, the enemy is thus perceived as the 'liberal' who, through federal state interventions (from school-busing to ordering the teaching of Darwinian evolution and perverse sexual practices), wants to undermine the authentic American way of life. The main economic idea deriving from this view is to get rid of the strong state, which taxes the hard-working population in order to finance its regulatory interventions; therefore the conservatives' minimal economic programme becomes 'fewer taxes, fewer regulations'.

From the standard perspective of the enlightened rational pursuit of self-interest, the inconsistency of this ideological stance is obvious: the populist conservatives are literally voting themselves into economic ruin. Less taxation and regulation means more freedom for the big companies that are driving impoverished farmers out of business; less state intervention means less federal help to small farmers, and so on. In the eyes of evangelical US populists, the state is an alien power and, together with international bodies like the UN, is an agent of the Antichrist: it takes away the liberty of the Christian believer, relieving him of the moral responsibility of stewardship, and in doing so undermines the individualistic morality that makes each of us the architect of our own salvation (though how to combine this with the unheard-of explosion of the state apparatuses under George W. Bush?). No wonder large corporations are delighted to accept these evangelical attacks on the state, especially when the state tries to regulate media mergers, to put strictures on energy companies, to strengthen air-pollution regulations, to protect wildlife and limit logging in the national parks, to name just a few interventions. It is the ultimate irony of history that radical individualism serves as the ideological justification for the unconstrained power of what the large majority of individuals experience as a vast anonymous network that, without any democratic public control, regulates their lives.

As to the ideological aspect of their struggle, it is more than obvious that the populist conservatives are fighting a war that simply cannot be won: if Republicans were effectively to ban abortion totally, if they were to prohibit the teaching of evolution, if they were to impose federal regulation on Hollywood and mass culture, this would mean not only their immediate ideological defeat, but also a large-scale economic depression in the US. The outcome is thus a debilitating symbiosis: although the 'ruling class' disagrees with the populists' moral agenda, it tolerates their 'moral war' as a means to keep the lower classes in check, i.e., to enable them to articulate their fury without disturbing the ruling classes' economic interests. What this means is that this 'culture war' is 'class war' in a displaced mode. So much for those who claim that we live in a post-class society.

This, however, makes the enigma only more impenetrable: how is this displacement possible? 'Stupidity' and 'ideological manipulation' are not answers: that is, it is clearly not enough to say that that the primitive lower classes are so brainwashed by ideological apparatuses that they are unable to identify their true interests. If nothing else, one should recall how, decades ago, the same Kansas was the hotbed of *progressive* populism in the US – and the people there certainly did not get more stupid in the last decades. Neither will a direct 'psychoanalytic' explanation in the old Wilhelm Reich style – people's libidinal investments compel them to act against their rational interests – serve: such an explanation brings together all too directly libidinal economy (unconscious desires) and economy proper, and thereby fails to grasp their mediation. It is also not enough to propose the Ernesto Laclau solution: that there is no 'natural' link between a given socio-economic position and the ideology attached to it – and therefore that it is meaningless to speak of 'deception' and 'false consciousness' as if there is somehow a standard of 'appropriate' ideological awareness inscribed into the very 'objective' socio-economic situation.[35] For Laclau, every ideological edifice is the outcome of a hegemonic fight to establish/impose a chain of equivalences, a fight whose outcome is thoroughly contingent, not guaranteed by any external reference like an 'objective socio-economic position'. Such a general answer explains everything without providing any specific explanation – the enigma (of acting against one's own interests) is not accounted for; it simply disappears.

The first thing to note here is that it takes two to fight a culture war. Culture is also the dominant ideological topic of the 'enlightened' liberals whose politics is focused on the fight against sexism, racism and fundamentalism and for multicultural tolerance. The key question is thus as follows: why is 'culture' emerging as our central life-world category? With regard to religion, we no longer 'really believe'; rather, we just follow (some of the) religious rituals and mores as part of the respect for the 'lifestyle' of the community to which we belong (non-believing Jews obeying kosher rules 'out of respect for tradition', and so on). 'I do not really believe in it, it is just part of my culture,' effectively seems to be the predominant mode of the disavowed/displaced belief that is characteristic of our times. What is a cultural lifestyle, if not the fact that, although we do not believe in Santa Claus, there is a Christmas tree in every house and even in public places every December? Perhaps, then, the 'non-fundamentalist' notion of 'culture' as distinguished from 'real' religion, art and so on is in its very core the name for the field of disowned/impersonal beliefs. 'Culture', in other words, is the name for all those things we practise without really believing in them, without 'taking them seriously'.

The second thing to note is how, while professing their solidarity with the poor, liberals encode their culture war with an opposed class message: more often than not, their fight for multicultural tolerance and women's rights marks the counter-position to the implied intolerance, fundamentalism and patriarchal sexism of the 'lower classes'. The way to unravel this confusion is to focus on the mediating terms, the function of which is to obfuscate the true lines of division. The way the term 'modernization' is used in the recent neoliberal ideological offensive is exemplary here. First, they construct an abstract opposition between 'modernizers' (those who endorse global capitalism in all its aspects, from economic to cultural) and 'traditionalists' (those who resist globalization). Into this category of those-who-resist are then thrown all, from the traditional conservatives and populist Right to the 'old Left' (those who continue to advocate the welfare state, trade unions, and so on). This categorization obviously does comprise an aspect of social reality – recall the coalition of Church and trade unions which, in Germany in early 2003, prevented the legalization of Sunday opening for shops. However, it is not enough to say that this 'cultural difference' traverses the entire social field, cutting across different strata and classes. It is not enough to say that this opposition can be combined in different ways with other oppositions (so that we can have the resistance of conservative 'traditional values' to global capitalist 'modernization', or moral conservatives who also fully endorse capitalist globalization). In short, it is not enough to say that this 'cultural difference' is one in the series of antagonisms that are operative in today's social processes. The failure of this opposition to provide the key to social totality does not only mean that one should take into account the complex interplay of all relevant social antagonisms. The wager of Marxism is that there is one antagonism ('class struggle') which overdetermines all others and which is as such the 'concrete universal' of the entire field. The term 'overdetermination' is here used in its precise Althusserian sense.

It does not mean that class struggle is the ultimate refer-
ent and horizon of meaning of all other struggles. It
means that class struggle is the structuring principle that
allows us to account for the very 'inconsistent' plurality of
ways in which other antagonisms can be articulated into
'chains of equivalences'. For example, feminist struggle can
be articulated into a chain with the progressive struggle for
emancipation, or it can (and it certainly does) function as
an ideological tool of the upper-middle classes to assert
their superiority over the 'patriarchal and intolerant' lower
classes. And the point here is not only that the feminist
struggle can be articulated in different ways within the class
antagonism, but that class antagonism is as it were doubly
inscribed here: it is the specific constellation of the class
struggle itself that explains why the feminist struggle was
appropriated by the upper-middle classes. (The same goes
for racism: it is the dynamics of class struggle itself that
explain why direct racism is strong among the lowest white
workers.) Class struggle is here the 'concrete universality' in
the strict Hegelian sense. In relating to its otherness (other
antagonisms), it relates to itself, which is to say that it (over-)
determines the way it relates to other struggles.

A similar class dynamics is at work in the Muslim
world. The Taliban are regularly presented as a fundamentalist Islamist group that enforces its rule through
terror. However, when, in the spring of 2009, the Taliban
took over Pakistan's Swat valley, the *New York Times*
reported that in order to do so they engineered 'a class
revolt that exploits profound fissures between a small
group of wealthy landlords and their landless tenants':

In Swat, accounts from those who have fled now make clear that the Taliban seized control by pushing out about four dozen landlords who held the most power. To do so, the militants organized peasants into armed gangs that became their shock troops ... The Taliban's ability to exploit class divisions adds a new dimension to the insurgency and is raising alarm about the risks to Pakistan, which remains largely feudal.[36]

The radical theologian Thomas Altizer has spelled out the implications and consequences of this new data (new to our Western ears) about the class content of the Taliban's appeal: 'Now', he observes,

> it is finally being revealed that the Taliban is a genuine liberating force assaulting an ancient feudal rule in Pakistan and freeing the vast peasant majority from that rule ... Hopefully we will now be given a genuine criticism of the Obama administration, which is far more dangerous than the Bush administration both because it is being given such a free hand and because it is a far stronger administration.[37]

The political consequence of this paradox is the properly dialectical tension between long-term strategy and short-term tactical alliances: although, in the long term, the very success of the radical-emancipatory struggle depends on mobilizing the lower classes that are today often in thrall to fundamentalist populism, one should have no problems with concluding short-term alliances with egalitarian liberals as part of the anti-sexist and anti-racist struggle.

The critique of European and American religious fundamentalism is an old topic with endless variations. The very pervasiveness of the self-satisfactory way in which liberals make fun of fundamentalists covers up the true problem: the hidden class dimension. And the same holds for the sentimental counterpart of this making-fun-of: the pathetic solidarity with the refugees and the no less false and pathetic self-humiliation of 'us' as by definition guilty of the predicament in which they find themselves. The task is to build bridges between 'our' and 'their' working class, engaging them in a struggle for solidarity. Without this unity (which includes the critique and self-critique of both sides), class struggle proper regresses into a clash of civilizations. That's why yet another taboo to be left behind is the dismissal of the worries and cares of so-called 'ordinary people' who are affected by the presence of refugees as an expression of racist prejudices – if not outright neo-Fascism. Should we really allow Pegida and co. to be the only option open to these people? Interestingly, the same motif seems to underlie the usual 'radical' Leftist critique of Bernie Sanders. As William Kaufman[38] has shown, what bothers Sanders' critics is precisely his close contact with small farmers and other working people in Vermont, the typical electoral supporters of Republican conservatives. Sanders is ready to listen to their worries and cares, rather than dismissing them as white racist trash.

Where Does the Threat
Come From?

Listening to ordinary people's worries, of course, in no way implies that one should accept the basic premise of their stance: the idea that the threat to their way of life comes from outside, from foreigners. The task is rather to teach them to recognize their own responsibility for the prospect of their destruction. To explain this point, let's take an example from another part of the world.

Udi Aloni's new film *Junction 48* deals with the difficult predicament of the young 'Israeli Palestinians' (Palestinians descended from the families that remained within Israel after the 1948 war), whose everyday life involves a continuous struggle on two fronts: against both Israeli state oppression and the fundamentalist pressures from within their own community. The main role is played by the well-known Israeli-Palestinian rapper Tamer Nafar, who, in his songs, mocks the tradition of 'honour killings' of girls in Palestinian families. Now, a strange thing happened to Nafar during a recent visit to the US. After he performed his song protesting against honour killings, at the Columbia University campus in New York, some anti-Zionist students attacked him for dealing with the topic – their reproach being that, in this way, he promotes the Zionist view of Palestinians as barbaric primitives (adding that, if there are indeed any honour killings, Israel is responsible for them because the Israeli occupation keeps Palestinians in primitive conditions and prevents their modernization). Here is Nafar's dignified reply: 'When you criticize me you criticize my own community in English to impress your radical professors. I sing in Arabic to protect the women in my own 'hood.'

What Nafar does in real life, as an artist, coincides here with the actions of his protagonist in the film: neither of them is protecting Palestinian girls from family terror in a patronizing way. Rather, they are allowing them to fight for themselves, and to take the risk of doing so. (At the end of Aloni's film, after the girl decides to perform at a concert against her family's wishes, her two brothers wait for her in a car in front of her house to carry out her killing. Although the film doesn't show what will happen, the impression is that the girl will be killed.)

In Spike Lee's film *Malcolm X* there is a wonderful detail: after Malcolm gives a talk at a college, a white student girl approaches him and asks him what she can do to help the black struggle. His answer is, 'Nothing.' The point of this answer is not that whites should just do nothing. Rather, they should first accept that black liberation should be the work of the blacks themselves, not something bestowed on them as a gift by the good white liberals, and only if they fully accept this fact can they do something to help the blacks. And herein resides Nafar's point as well: Palestinians do not need the patronizing help of Western liberals; even less do they need the silence about honour killing that is part of the Western Leftist's 'respect' for the Palestinian way of life. These two aspects – the imposition of Western values as universal human rights, and the respect for different cultures independently of the horrors that can be part of these cultures – are the two sides of the same ideological mystification. A lot has been written about how the universality of universal human rights is twisted, how they secretly give preference to Western cultural values and norms (the priority of the individual over his/her community, and so on).[39] But we should also add to this insight that the multiculturalist anti-colonialist defence of the multiplicity of 'ways of life' is also false: it covers up the antagonisms within each of these particular ways of life, justifying acts of brutality, sexism and racism as expressions of a particular culture that we have no right to judge by foreign 'Western values'. Here is a typical anti-colonialist defence of specific ways of life used as a justification of brutal homophobia – Robert Mugabe's talk at the UN General Assembly on 28 September 2015:

Respecting and upholding human rights is the obligation of all states, and is enshrined in the United Nations charter. Nowhere does the charter abrogate the right to some to sit in judgment over others, in carrying out this universal obligation. In that regard, we reject the politicization of this important issue and the application of double standards to victimize those who dare think and act independently of the self-anointed prefects of our time. We equally reject attempts to prescribe 'new rights' that are contrary to our values, norms, traditions, and beliefs. We are not gays! Cooperation and respect for each other will advance the cause of human rights world-wide. Confrontation, vilification, and double-standards will not.[40]

(A couple of months earlier, Mugabe described homosexuals as 'worse than pigs, goats and birds'.[41]) What can Mugabe's emphatic claim 'We are not gays!' mean with regard to the fact that, for certain, there *are* many gays in Zimbabwe? It means, of course, that in Mugabe's Zimbabwe gays are reduced to an oppressed minority whose acts are often directly criminalized. But one can understand Mugabe's underlying logic: the gay movement is perceived as an expression of the cultural impact of capitalist globalization and of its undermining of traditional social and cultural forms, so that, consequently, the struggle against gays appears as an aspect of the anti-colonial struggle. Does the same not hold for, say, Boko Haram? For its members, the liberation of women appears as the most visible feature of the destructive cultural impact of capitalist modernization, so that Boko Haram (whose name can be roughly and descriptively translated as 'Western education is forbidden', specifically the education of women) can perceive and portray itself as an agent fighting the destructive impact of modernization, by way of imposing a hierarchic regulation of the relationship between the sexes. The enigma is thus: why do Muslims, who have undoubtedly been exposed to exploitation, domination, and other destructive and humiliating aspects of colonialism, target in their response what is (for us, at least) the best part of the Western legacy: our egalitarianism and personal freedoms, inclusive of a healthy dose of irony and a mocking of all authorities? The obvious answer is that their target is well-chosen. What for them makes the liberal West so unbearable is not only that it practises exploitation and violent domination but that, to add insult to injury, it presents this brutal reality in the guise of its opposite: freedom, equality and democracy.

Mugabe's regressive defence of particular ways of life finds its mirror-image in the actions of Viktor Orban, the Rightist prime minister of Hungary. In autumn 2015 he justified closing the border with Serbia as the defending of Christian Europe against invading Muslims. Is this the same Orban who, back in the summer of 2012, said that in Central Europe a new economic system must be built, and

> let us hope that God will help us and we will not have to invent a new type of political system instead of democracy that would need to be introduced for the sake of economic survival [. . .] Cooperation is a question of force, not of intention. Perhaps there are countries where things don't work that way, for example in the Scandinavian countries, but such a half-Asiatic rag-tag people as we are can unite only if there is force.[42]

The irony of these lines was not lost on some old Hungarian dissidents. When in 1956 the Soviet army moved into Budapest to crush the anti-Communist uprising, the message repeatedly sent by the beleaguered Hungarian leaders to the West was: 'We are defending Europe here.' (Against the Asiatic Communists, of course.) Now, after the collapse of Communism, Hungary's Christian-conservative government paints as its main enemy Western multicultural consumerist liberal democracy, for which today's Western Europe stands, and calls for a new more organic communitarian order to replace the 'turbulent' liberal democracy of the last two decades. Orban has already expressed his sympathies with the 'capitalism with Asian values', so, if the European pressure on Orban continues, we can easily imagine him sending a message to the East along these lines: 'We are defending Asia here!' (And – to add an ironic twist – from the West European racist perspective, are not today's Hungarians the descendants of the early medieval Huns? Attila is even today a popular Hungarian name.)

Is there a contradiction between these two Orbans: Orban the friend of Putin who resents the liberal-democratic West, and Orban the defender of Christian Europe? There is none. The two faces of Orban provide the proof (if it were needed) that the principal threat to Europe does not come in the shape of Muslim immigrants but in its anti-immigrant populist defenders.

So, what if Europe should accept the paradox that its democratic openness is based on exclusion: there is 'no freedom for the enemies of freedom', as Robespierre put it long ago? In principle, this is of course a reasonable proposition, but it is here that one has to be very specific. In a way, the Norwegian terrorist Breivik was right in his choice of target: he didn't attack foreigners but those within his own community who were too tolerant towards the intruders. The problem is not foreigners, it is our own (European) identity. Although the ongoing crisis of the European Union appears as one of economy and finance, it is, fundamentally, an *ideologico-political* crisis. The failure of referendums on the EU constitution in France and the Netherlands in 2005 gave a clear signal that voters perceived the EU as a 'technocratic' economic union, one lacking any vision that could mobilize people: until the recent wide protest movements in Greece and Spain, the only ideology able to inspire action was the anti-immigrant defence of Europe (or the defence of UK borders, in the case of Britain).

In order to really undermine the notion of the defence of the European 'homeland' against foreign threat, one should reject its very presupposition: namely that every ethnic group has its own proper Nativia. On 7 September 2015, Sarah Palin gave an interview to Fox News, in which she tells *Fox and Friends* host Steve Doocy:

I love immigrants. But like Donald Trump, I just think we have too darn many in this country. Mexican-Americans, Asian-Americans, Native-Americans – they're changing up the cultural mix in the United States away from what it used to be in the days of our Founding Fathers. I think we should go to some of these groups and just ask politely – would you mind going home? Would you mind giving us our country back?'

'Sarah, you know I love you,' Doocy interjects, 'and I think that's a great idea with regards to Mexicans. But where are the Native Americans supposed to go? They don't really have a place to go back to, do they?' Sarah replies:

> Well, I think they should go back to Nativia or wherever they came from. The liberal media treats Native Americans like they're gods. As if they just have some sort of automatic right to be in this country. But I say if they can't learn to get off those horses and start speaking American – then they should be sent home too.[43]

Unfortunately, we immediately learned that this story – too good to be true – is a hoax, brilliantly performed by the *Daily Currant*. However, *se non è vero, è ben trovato*, as they say; it was nonetheless a fake which hit the mark. In its ridiculous nature, it brought out the hidden fantasy that sustains the anti-immigrant vision: in today's chaotic global world, there is a Nativia to which people who bother us properly belong. This vision was realized in apartheid South Africa in the form of 'Bantustans', territories set aside for black inhabitants. The long-term goal was to make the Bantustans independent – as a result, blacks would lose their South African citizenship and voting rights, allowing whites to remain in control of South Africa. Although Bantustans were defined as the 'original homes' of the black peoples of South Africa, different black groups were allocated to their homelands in a brutally arbitrary way: these Bantustans amounted to 13 per cent of the country's land, carefully selected so as not to contain any important mineral deposits, the remainder being reserved for the white population. The process was completed by the Bantu Homelands Citizenship Act of 1970, which formally designated all black South Africans as citizens of the homelands, even if they lived in 'white South Africa', and cancelled their South African citizenship. From the apartheid standpoint, this solution was ideal. Whites possessed most of the land, and blacks were proclaimed foreigners in their own country, treated as guest workers who could be deported at any point back to their 'homeland'. What cannot but strike the eye is the artificial nature of this entire process. Black groups were suddenly told that an unattractive and infertile piece of land was their 'true home'. And even if a Palestinian state were to emerge on the West Bank, would it not be precisely such a Bantustan, its formal 'independence' serving the purpose of liberating the Israeli government from any responsibility for the welfare of the people living there?

The Limits of Neighbourhood

To understand fully the deepest background of our troubled relationship with neighbours, one should take a closer philosophical look at the notion of the Neighbour. As Adam Kotsko has shown in his book *Creepiness*, 'creepy' is today's name for the uncanny core of a neighbour: every neighbour is ultimately creepy. What makes a neighbour creepy are not his weird acts but the impenetrability of the desire that sustains these acts. For example, the creepiness of Marquis de Sade's writing is not primarily its content (which is rather dull and repetitive) but 'why is he doing it?' Everything in Sade is a 'sadist' perversion, everything except his writing, the act of its creation, which cannot be accounted for as a perversion. So the question is: What does a creepy neighbour want? What does he get out of it? An experience, an encounter, gets creepy when we all of a sudden suspect that he is doing something for a motive other than the obvious one.

The onset of the post-'68 hedonist permissiveness that was part of the prospect of integrating nations into larger communities held together by the global market did not give rise to universal tolerance but, on the contrary, triggered a new wave of racist segregation: 'Our future as common markets will be balanced by an increasingly hard-line extension of the process of segregation.'[44] Why?

Those who understand globalization as an opportunity for the entire earth to be a unified space of communication, one which brings together all humanity, often fail to notice this dark side of their proposition. Since a Neighbour is, as Freud suspected long ago, primarily a Thing, a traumatic intruder, someone whose different way of life (or, rather, way of *jouissance* materialized in its social practices and rituals) disturbs us and, when the Neighbour comes too close, throws the balance of our way of life off the rails, this can also give rise to an aggressive reaction aimed at getting rid of this disturbing intruder. As Peter Sloterdijk puts it: 'At first, more communication means, above all, more conflict.'[45] This is why Sloterdijk is right to claim that the attitude of 'understanding-each-other' has to be supplemented by the attitude of 'getting-out-of-each-other's-way', by maintaining an appropriate distance, by implementing a new 'code of discretion'. European civilization finds it easier to tolerate different ways of life precisely on account of what its critics usually denounce as its weakness and failure, namely the alienation of social life. One of the things alienation means is that distance is woven into the very social texture of everyday life: even if I live side by side with others, in my normal state I ignore them. I am allowed not to get too close to others. I move in a social space where I interact with others obeying certain external 'mechanical' rules, without sharing their inner world. Perhaps the lesson to be learned is that, sometimes, a dose of alienation is indispensable for the peaceful coexistence of ways of life. Sometimes *alienation* is not a problem but a solution.

Sometimes, alienation is like alcohol for Homer Simpson: 'the cause of, and solution to, all life's problems'!

What, then, is the factor that renders different cultures (or, rather, ways of life in the rich complexity of their daily practices) incompatible, what is the obstacle that prevents their fusion or, at least, their harmoniously indifferent co-existence? The psychoanalytic answer is: *jouissance* (Lacan's term designating excessive pleasure coinciding with pain). It is not only that different modes of *jouissance* are incongruous with each other, without a common measure; the other's *jouissance* is insupportable for us because (and insofar as) we cannot find a proper way to relate to our own *jouissance* – the ultimate incompatibility is not between mine and other's *jouissance*, but between myself and my own *jouissance*, which forever remains an ex-timate intruder. It is to resolve this deadlock that the subject projects the core of its *jouissance* onto an Other, attributing to this Other full access to a consistent *jouissance*. Such a constellation cannot but give rise to jealousy: in jealousy, the subject creates or imagines a paradise (a utopia of full *jouissance*) from which he is excluded. The same definition applies to what one can call political jealousy: from the anti-Semitic fantasies about the excessive enjoyment of the Jews to the Christian fundamentalists' fantasies about the weird sexual practices of gays and lesbians.

When Freud and Lacan insist on the problematic nature of the basic Judeo-Christian injunction to love one's neighbour, they are thus not just making the standard critico-ideological point about how every notion of universality is coloured by our particular values and in this way implies secret exclusions. They are making a much stronger point about the incompatibility of the idea of the Neighbour with the very dimension of universality. What resists universality is the properly *inhuman* dimension of the Neighbour. The humanist universality that is condemned to failure is the universality of fellow men who recognize themselves in others, i.e. who 'know' that beneath all our political and religious passions we are all the same, sharing the same fears and emotions . . .

The same strategy of ideological 'humanization' ('rendering-human' in the sense, for example, of the proverbial wisdom 'to err is human') is a key constituent of the ideological (self-)presentation of the Israeli Defense Forces. The Israeli media love to dwell on the imperfections and psychic traumas of the Israeli soldiers, presenting them neither as perfect military machines nor as over-human heroes, but as ordinary people who, caught in the traumas of history and warfare, commit errors and can get lost like all normal people do. When, in January 2003, the Israeli Defense Forces demolished the house of the family of a 'suspected terrorist', they did so with accentuated kindness, even helping the family to move their furniture out before destroying the house with a bulldozer. A similar incident was reported a short time before in the Israeli press. And when an Israeli soldier was searching a Palestinian house for suspects, the mother of the family called her daughter by her name in order to calm her down, and the surprised soldier learned that the frightened girl's name was the same as that of his own daughter; in a sentimental upsurge, he pulled out his wallet and showed her picture to the Palestinian mother. It is easy to discern the falsity of such a gesture of empathy: the notion that, in spite of political differences, we are all human beings with the same loves and worries, neutralizes the impact of what the soldier is effectively doing at that moment. So, the only proper reply of the mother would be: 'If you really are human like me, why are you doing what you are doing now?' The soldier could then take refuge only in reified duty – 'I don't like it, but it is my duty' – thereby avoiding the subjective assumption of his duty. The message of such humanization is to emphasize the gap between the complex reality of the person and the role he has to play against his true nature: 'In my family, genetic is not military,' as one of the interviewed soldiers says in Claude Lanzmann's *Tsahal*.

Does this mean that we are constrained to cultural relativism, that there is no universal human dimension? No, but this universal dimension is to be sought beyond sympathy and understanding, beyond the 'we're all human' level: at another level, which should be designated precisely as that of the *inhuman* Neighbour. Let us illustrate this key point with a perhaps unexpected example. As Robert Pippin has shown in his perspicacious reading of John Ford's film *The Searchers*, this move towards the abyss of the Neighbour is what happens in the crucial scene towards the end, when Ethan finally gets hold of Debbie (who has spent years as a captive of Comanches) and runs after her. Throughout the film, his explicit intent is not to save her and bring her home, but to kill her: he is motivated by the racist idea that a white girl who has lived with Indians becomes a worthless outcast and deserves only to die. Holding Debbie in his hands, he raises her up, embraces her and decides to take her home. Where did this change come from? The standard explanation is that, at the vital moment, Ethan's deep goodness takes over. Pippin, however, rejects this reading. He focuses on a strange shot of Ethan's (John Wayne's) face just before he gets hold of Debbie, when he sees her running away from him. Ethan's gaze, Pippin notes, does not express some reawakened human warmth and sympathy. Rather,

> the primary expression here is *puzzlement*, some indication that Ethan does not know his own mind and suddenly realizes he does not know his own mind ... What we and he discover is that he did not know his own mind well, that he avowed principles that were partly confabulations and fantasy. We (and he) find out the depth and extent of his actual commitments only when he finally must act.[46]

One can therefore say that, at the moment of the strange shot of Ethan's perplexed face, Ethan discovers himself as a Neighbour, in the impenetrable abyss of his subjectivity. When he finally finds himself in the position to act upon this self-identity, he confronts the undecidable enigma of his personality that is undermining his identity as the 'Ethan' onto which he (and we, the film's spectators) have been fixed: a man obsessed by a murderous commitment to securing Debbie's redemption through killing her. The link with universality is clear here: Ethan accepts Debbie not by 'finally understanding her', getting an empathetic insight into how she must have experienced her predicament, but by realizing that he does not understand even himself, that he is also a stranger to himself.

Universality is a universality of 'strangers', of individuals reduced to the abyss of impenetrability in relation not only to others but also to themselves. When dealing with foreigners, we should always bear in mind Hegel's concise formula: the secrets of the ancient Egyptians were secret also for the Egyptians themselves. That's why the privileged way to reach a Neighbour is not that of empathy, of trying to understand them, but a disrespectful laughter which makes fun both of them and of us in our mutual lack of (self-)understanding (inclusive of 'racist' jokes).

And we should ruthlessly apply this insight also to the poor; more precisely, on the attempts of the well-off to 'understand' the poor, to learn how it feels to be poor. Alenka Zupančič develops this point succinctly apropos Preston Sturges's *Sullivan's Travels* (1941), a movie directly dealing with the limits of 'understanding the poor'. Sturges

frontally dismantles the axiom 'poor is good', as well as the condescending posture relating to it. And, philosophically most interestingly, he proposes a kind of *ontology of poverty*. I am referring to the deservingly famous exchange between Sullivan and his valet Burrows, when the latter learns that Sullivan wants to get out there to experience poverty and deprivation first hand, so as to make a better and more realistic movie about it. Here are some bits of the dialogue:

Sullivan: I'm going out on the road to find out what it's like to be poor and needy and then I'm going to make a picture about it.

Burrows: If you'll permit me to say so, sir, the subject is not an interesting one. The poor know all about poverty and only the morbid rich would find the topic glamorous.

Sullivan: But I'm doing it for the poor. Don't you understand?

[. . .]

Burrows: You see, sir, rich people and theorists – who are usually rich people – think of poverty in the negative, as the lack of riches – as disease might be called the lack of health. But it isn't, sir. Poverty is not the lack of anything, but a positive plague, virulent in itself, contagious as cholera, with filth, criminality, vice and despair as only a few of its symptoms. It is to be stayed away from, even for purposes of study.

This is an amazing speech, a speech that we should repeat and recite today with rigour, in the face of the (exclusively) humanitarian approach to poverty and of its sentimentalization. There is absolutely nothing glamorous or 'nice' about poverty, and we should not think of it simply in negative terms: it is an ontological entity of its own standing. Poverty does not simply mean to have little or no money; it is not reducible to the description of one's miserable circumstances.

As much as a good-hearted rich man may want to think that underneath all his wealth, he is just the same kind of human being as the poor are, *he is wrong*. Once we have our social (class) positions, there is no zero-level of humanity where we are all the same. He is not one of them: they are not in the same boat, and it would be extremely presumptuous to think so.[47]

Sturges engages here in an implicit polemic with Frank Capra, the director whose work can be conceived as a long variation on the motif of the supposed 'goodness' of the (poor) neighbour. As the critic James Harvey writes:

Capra seems nearly unable to imagine a poor person who isn't genteel, once you get to know him. Getting to know him is always the main problem – as it is with your neighbor, too. John Doe sees 'the answer' – 'the only thing capable of saving this cockeyed world' resides in people's 'finally learning that the guy next door isn't a bad egg.' But what if you learn that he *is* – even worse than you imagined, or at least more troublesome? Then what? – forget him?[48]

And exactly the same holds for refugees. What if 'getting to know them' reveals that they are more or less like us – impatient, violent, demanding – *plus*, usually, part of a culture that cannot accept many of the features we perceive as self-evident? One should therefore cut the link between refugees and humanitarian empathy, in which we ground our help to refugees in our compassion for their suffering. We should, rather, help them because it is our ethical duty to do so, because we cannot not do it if we want to remain decent people, but without any of the sentimentalism that breaks down the moment we realize that most of the refugees are *not* 'people like us' (not because they are foreigners, but because *we* ourselves are not 'people like us'). To paraphrase Winston Churchill: 'Sometimes doing the good is not enough, even if it is the best you can do. Sometimes you must do what is required.' It is not enough to do (what we consider to be) the best for the refugees, receive them with open hands, show sympathy and generosity to the utmost of our ability. The very fact that such displays of generosity make us feel good should make us suspicious: are we not doing this to forget what is required?

Hateful Thousands in Cologne

Who are the 'hateful eight' in Quentin Tarantino's film of the same name? The *entire* group of participants – white racists and the black Union soldier, men and women, law officers and criminals – all are equally mean, brutal and revengeful. The most embarrassing moment in the film occurs when the black officer (played by the superb Samuel L. Jackson) narrates in detail and with obvious pleasure to an old Confederate general how he killed the general's racist son, who had been responsible for many black deaths: after forcing him to march naked in cold winds, Jackson promises the freezing man he will get a warm covering if he performs fellatio; the deed done, Jackson reneges on his promise and lets him die. So there are no good guys in the struggle against racism: they are all engaged in it with utmost brutality. And is the lesson of the recent Cologne sex attacks not uncannily similar to the lesson of the film? Even if (most of) the refugees are effectively victims fleeing from ruined countries, this does not prevent some of them from acting in a despicable way. We tend to forget that there is nothing redemptive in suffering: being a victim at the bottom of the social ladder does not make you some kind of privileged voice of morality and justice, as we saw earlier in Ruth Klüger's example.

But this general insight is not enough – one has to take a close look at the situation that gave birth to the Cologne incident. In his analysis of the global situation after the Paris bombings,[49] Alain Badiou discerns three predominant types of subjectivity in today's global capitalism: the Western 'civilized' middle-class liberal-democratic subject; those outside the West possessed by the 'desire for the West/*le désir d'Occident*,' desperately endeavouring to imitate the 'civilized' lifestyle of the Western middle classes; and the Fascist nihilists, those whose envy of the West turns into a mortal self-destructive hatred. Badiou makes it clear that what the media call the 'radicalization' of Muslims is Fascistization pure and simple:

> this Fascism is the obverse of the frustrated desire for the West which is organized in a more or less military way following the flexible model of a mafia gang and with variable ideological colorizations where the place occupied by religion is purely formal.(47)

In his (otherwise outstanding) analysis of the logic that sustains ISIS terrorist attacks, Jean-Claude Milner rejects the designation of ISIS as Fascist: 'The word "Fascism" is always mentioned with regard to the massacre of January 9. Nothing could be more inappropriate. Religion plays no decisive role in Fascism.'[50] In this specific case, though, Badiou is nonetheless right in applying the term to both Muslim and Christian fundamentalist terror. His point is that religion is *not* a decisive factor with ISIS; it merely serves as a medium for the perverted expression of disavowed class envy and hatred – and Fascism feeds precisely on such a frustration.

Western middle-class ideology has two opposing features: it displays an arrogant belief in the superiority of its values (universal human rights and freedoms); but, simultaneously, it is obsessed by the fear that its limited domain will be invaded by billions who are outside, who do not count in global capitalism since they are neither producing commodities nor consuming them. The fear of the members of this middle class is that they will end up in the ranks of those thus excluded. The clearest expression of this 'desire for the West' is represented by immigrant refugees: their desire is not a revolutionary one, it is the desire to leave behind their devastated habitat and rejoin the promised land of the developed West. (Those who remain behind try to create there miserable copies of Western prosperity, like the 'modernized' parts in every Third World metropolis, in Luanda, Lagos, and so on, with Italian-style cafés, shopping malls, etc.)

But since, for the large majority of pretenders, this desire cannot be satisfied, one of the remaining options is the nihilist reversal: frustration and envy get radicalized into a murderous and self-destructive hatred of the West, and people become involved in violent revenge. Badiou declares this violence to be a pure expression of the death drive, a violence that can only culminate in acts of orgiastic (self-) destruction, without any serious vision of an alternative society. Badiou is right to emphasize that there is no emancipatory potential in fundamentalist violence, however anti-capitalist it claims to be: it is a phenomenon strictly inherent to the global capitalist universe, its 'hidden phantom' (43). The basic fact of fundamentalist Fascism is envy. Fundamentalism remains rooted in the *desire* for the West in its very *hatred* of the West. We are dealing here with the standard reversal of frustrated desire into aggressiveness described by psychoanalysis; here, Islam simply provides the form to ground this (self-)destructive hatred. This destructive potential of envy is the base of Rousseau's well-known, but nonetheless not fully exploited, distinction between egotism, *amour-de-soi* (that love of the self which is natural), and *amour-propre*, the perverted preferring of oneself to others in which a person focuses not on achieving a goal, but on destroying the obstacle to it:

> The primitive passions, which all directly tend towards our happiness, make us deal only with objects which relate to them, and whose principle is only amour-de-soi, are all in their essence lovable and tender; however, when, *diverted from their objects by obstacles, they are more occupied with the obstacle they try to get rid of, than with the object they try to reach,* they change their nature and become irascible and hateful. This is how amour-de-soi, which is a noble and absolute feeling, becomes amour-propre, that is to say, a relative feeling by means of which one compares oneself, a feeling which demands preferences, *whose enjoyment is purely negative and which does not strive to find satisfaction in our own well-being, but only in the misfortune of others.*[51]

An evil person is thus *not* an egotist, 'thinking only about his own interests'. A true egotist is too busy taking care of his own good to have time to cause misfortune to others. The primary vice of a bad person is precisely that he is more preoccupied with others than with himself. Rousseau is describing a precise libidinal mechanism: the inversion which generates the shift of the libidinal investment from the object to the obstacle itself. This could well be applied to fundamentalist violence – be it the Oklahoma bombing or 9/11. In both cases, we are dealing with hatred pure and simple: destroying the obstacle – the Oklahoma City Federal Building, the Twin Towers – was what really mattered, not achieving the noble goal of a truly Christian or Muslim society.[52] Such a Fascistization can exert a certain pull on the frustrated immigrant youth, who cannot find a proper place in Western societies or a future with which to identify. Fascistization offers them an easy way out of their frustration: an eventful, risky life dressed up in a sacrificial religious dedication, plus material satisfaction (sex, cars, weapons). One should not forget that Islamic State is also a big mafia trading company selling oil, ancient statues, cotton, arms and women-slaves, 'a mixture of deadly heroic propositions and, simultaneously, of Western corruption by products' (48).

It goes without saying that not everything fundamentalist terrorists do can be filed under the category of self-destructive nihilism. For example, some recently disclosed ISIS documents indicate some reasons for the Paris bombings: what may appear to us a reason against – bombings definitely mean troubles for the millions of Muslims living in France – may be the very reason for them. That is to say, what ISIS wants to achieve is the elimination, as far as possible, of the 'moderate Western Muslim' demographic, and to radicalize them, so that conditions will be created for an open civil war. And one should also note that this goal greatly overlaps with the goal of anti-immigrant racists – they both want a full and unequivocal 'clash of civilizations'. But the same final outcome is nevertheless reached in this roundabout way: nihilist self-destruction.[53]

It is also the case that this fundamentalist-Fascist violence is just one of the many modes of violence that pertains to global capitalism itself: from the catastrophic consequences of the globalized economy to the long story of Western military intervention. Islamo-Fascism is a profoundly reactive phenomenon, in the Nietzschean sense of the term: an expression of impotence converted into self-destructive rage. So, while agreeing with the overall thrust of Badiou's analysis, I find problematic three of its claims. First, the reduction of the role of religion in Fascist nihilism to a secondary superficial feature: 'religion is only a clothing, it is in no way the heart of the matter, only a form of subjectivization, not the real content of the thing.' (46) Badiou is totally right in his claim that the search for the roots of today's Muslim terrorism in ancient religious texts (the 'it is all already in the Qur'an' argument) is misleading: one should instead focus on today's global capitalism, and understand Islamo-Fascism as one of the modes of reaction to its lure, by way of inverting envy into hatred. But from a critical standpoint, is not religion always a kind of clothing, not the heart of the matter? Is not religion in its very core a 'form of subjectivization' of people's predicaments? And, in turn, does this not imply that such clothing *is* in some sense the 'heart of the matter', the way individuals experience their situation: there is no way for them to step out of their world and somehow see, from 'outside', how things 'really are'? Ideology does not reside primarily in stories invented (by those in power) to deceive others, it resides in stories invented by subjects to deceive themselves. Then, there is Badiou's identification of refugees and migrants with a 'nomadic proletariat' (61), a 'virtual vanguard of the gigantic mass of the people whose existence is not counted [*prise en compte*] in the world the way it is' (62). But are migrants (most of them, at least) not those among the Third World population who are most strongly possessed by the 'desire for the West', most strongly in the thrall of hegemonic ideology, and as such most resistant to proletarian identification and therefore to playing the role of a 'vanguard' to the 'mass of the people'? Finally, there is the naive demand that we should

> go and see who is this other about whom one talks, who are they really. We have to gather their thoughts, their ideas, their vision of things, and inscribe them, and ourselves simultaneously, into a strategic vision of the fate of humanity' (63).

Easy to say, difficult to do. This other is, as Badiou himself shows, utterly disoriented, possessed by the opposing attitudes of envy and hatred, a hatred that ultimately expresses its own repressed desire for the West (which is why hatred turns into self-destruction). It is part of a naive humanist metaphysics to presuppose that, beneath this vicious cycle of desire, envy and hatred, there is some 'deeper' human core of global solidarity. Stories abound about how, among the refugees, many Syrians are an exception: in transition camps they clean up after themselves, they behave in a polite and respectful way, many of them are well-educated and speak English, they often even pay for what they consume . . . In short, they are like ourselves, our educated and civilized middle classes. (And they even try to establish solidarity with indigenous Europeans: in Slovenia, the media reported cases of Syrian middle-class immigrants, when conversing with the Slovenes who were helping them, warning them against the majority of other refugees, whom they described as brutal and primitive.)

It is popular to claim that the violent refugees represent a minority, and that the large majority has a deep respect for women. While this is of course true, one should nonetheless cast a closer look into the structure of such respect: what kind of woman is 'respected', and what is expected from her in this regard? What if a woman is 'respected' insofar (and only insofar) as she fits the ideal of a docile servant faithfully doing her home chores, so that her man has the right to explode in fury if she instead 'goes viral' and acts in full autonomy?

Our media usually contrasts 'civilized' middle-class refugees with 'barbarian' lower-class refugees who steal, harass our citizens, behave violently towards women, defecate in public (or so we are told). Instead of dismissing all this as racist propaganda, one should gather the courage to discern a moment of truth in it: traditionally, in resisting those in power, one of the strategies of the 'lower classes' has been to use terrifying displays of carnivalesque brutality to disturb the middle-class sense of decency. And one is tempted to read the events on New Year's Eve in Cologne in this way – as an obscene lower-class carnival:

> German police are investigating reports that scores of women were sexually assaulted and mugged in Cologne city centre during New Year's Eve celebrations, in what a minister called a 'completely new dimension of crime'. According to the police, those allegedly responsible for the sex attacks and numerous robberies were of Arab and North African origin. Over 100 complaints were filed to police, a third of which were linked to sexual assault. The city centre turned into a 'lawless zone': between 500 and 1000 men described as drunk and aggressive are believed to have been behind the attacks on partygoers in the centre of the western German city. Whether they were working as a single group or in separate gangs remains unclear. Women reported being tightly surrounded by groups of men who harassed and mugged them. Some people threw fireworks into the crowds, adding to the chaos. One of the victims had been raped. A volunteer policewoman was among those said to have been sexually assaulted.[54]

As expected, this phenomenon is growing: not just in terms of more and more women – now over 500 – coming forward to file complaints, but also of similar incidents in other German – and indeed Swedish – cities. There are even indications that the attacks were coordinated in advance. What's more, right-wing anti-immigrant 'defenders of the civilized West' are striking back with attacks on immigrants, so that the spiral of violence threatens to intensify. And, as expected, the Politically Correct liberal Left mobilizes its resources to downplay the incident, in much the same way it did in the Rotherham case not so long ago. In Cologne the liberal Left misses the key dimension of the event: the Cologne carnival should be located in the long line of cases reaching back to 1730s Paris, to the so-called 'Great Cat Massacre', described by Robert Darnton,[55] when a group of printing apprentices tortured and ritually killed all the cats they could find, including the pet of their master's wife. The apprentices, habitually,

> slept in a filthy freezing room, rose before dawn, ran errands all day while dodging insults from the journeymen and abuse from the master, and received nothing but slops to eat. They found the food especially galling. Instead of dining at the master's table, they had to eat scraps from his plate in the kitchen. Worse still, the cook secretly sold the leftovers and gave the boys cat food – old, rotten bits of meat that they could not stomach and so passed on to the cats, who refused it.

So they were literally treated worse than the cats adored by the master's wife, especially *la grise* (the grey), her favourite.

A passion for cats seemed to have swept through the printing trade, at least at the level of the masters, or bourgeois as the workers called them. One bourgeois kept twenty-five cats. He had their portraits painted and fed them on roast fowl.

One night the boys resolved to right this inequitable state of affairs. Armed with broomhandles, printing-press bars and other tools of their trade, they went after every cat they could find, beginning with *la grise*. Their gang-leader smashed its spine with an iron bar and finished it off, then they stashed it in a gutter while the journeymen drove the other cats across the rooftops, bludgeoning all within reach and trapping in sacks those who tried to escape. They dumped sack-loads of half-dead cats in the courtyard, and the entire workshop gathered round and staged a mock trial, complete with guards, confessor and a public executioner. After pronouncing the animals guilty and administering last rites, they strung them up on an improvised gallows, the men delirious with joy, disorder, and laughter. How could they find such a repulsive ritual so enjoyable? 'Where is the humour in a group of grown men bleating like goats and banging with their tools while an adolescent re-enacts the ritual slaughter of a defenseless animal?'

The cat massacre obviously served as an indirect attack on the master and his wife, and expressed the workers' hatred for the bourgeois: the masters love cats; consequently the workers hate them. Cats occupied an exalted position in the bourgeois way of life, while keeping pets was as alien to the workers as torturing animals was to the bourgeois. Trapped between incompatible sensitivities, the cats had the worst of both worlds. By executing the cats with such elaborate ceremony, the printers declared the master guilty: guilty of overworking and underfeeding his apprentices, guilty of living in luxury while his journeymen did all the work, guilty of withdrawing from the shop instead of labouring and eating with the men, as the masters were said to have done a generation or two earlier. The guilt extended from the boss to the whole system. Perhaps in trying, confessing and hanging a collection of half-dead cats, the workers meant to ridicule the entire legal and social order. A half-century later, the artisans of Paris would run riot in a similar manner, combining indiscriminate slaughter with improvised popular tribunals. It would be absurd to view the cat massacre as a dress rehearsal for the September massacres of the French Revolution, but the earlier outburst of violence did suggest a popular rebellion, though it remained restricted to the level of symbolism.

But why was the killing so funny? During traditional carnival the common people suspended the normal rules of behaviour and ceremoniously reversed the social order or turned it upside down in riotous procession. Carnival was high season for hilarity, sexuality and youth run riot, and the crowd often incorporated cat torture into its rough music. While mocking a cuckold or some other victim, the youths passed around a cat, tearing its fur to make it howl. *Faire le chat*, they called it. The Germans called it *Katzenmusik*, a term that may have been derived from the howls of tortured cats. The torture of animals, especially cats, was a popular amusement throughout early modern Europe. The power of cats was concentrated on the most intimate aspect of domestic life: sex. *Le chat*, *la chatte*, *le minet* mean the same thing in French slang as 'pussy' does in English, and they have served as obscenities for centuries.

So, what if we conceive of the Cologne incident as a contemporary version of *faire le chat*? As a carnivalesque rebellion of the underdogs? It wasn't the simple urge for satisfaction of sexually starved young men – that could be done in a more discreet, hidden way – it was foremost a public spectacle of instilling fear and humiliation, of exposing the privileged Germans to painful helplessness. There is, of course, nothing redemptive or emancipatory, nothing effectively liberating, in such a carnival – but this is how actual carnivals work. And what this carnivalesque enjoyment means is that nobody is merely a victim in this situation. It is true that the West (especially the old colonizers, England and France, and later the US) long ago began to sow the wind – through brutal colonial interventions, etc. – and are today reaping the whirlwind. However, their Arab victims also share their part of responsibility for the carnivalesque brutality: what makes them guilty is the way they subjectivized their predicament by way of engaging in nihilist (self-)destruction and obscene aggressiveness – we are always fully responsible for the way we enjoy ourselves.

This is why the naive attempts to enlighten immigrants (explaining to them that our sexual mores are different, that a woman who walks in public in a miniskirt and smiles does not thereby signal sexual invitation, and so on) are examples of breathtaking stupidity. Immigrants know all this perfectly well – and that's why they are doing it. They are well aware that what they are doing is foreign to our predominant culture, and they are doing it precisely to wound our sensitivities. The task is not to teach them what they already know very well, but to change this stance of envy and revengeful aggressiveness. We often hear that the struggle for women's rights and the struggle against anti-immigrant racism is the same struggle – those who worry about attacks on women should also worry about attacks on refugees – true, but it also works the other way: how do we make those among the refugees who attack women accept that the struggle against what they are doing in this specific instance is also the struggle for their own rights?

The difficult lesson of this entire affair is therefore that it is not enough simply to give voice to the underdogs as they are now: in order to enact actual emancipation, they have to be *educated* (by others and by themselves) into their freedom – an almost impossible task in the darkness that is growing all around Europe and the Middle East. Western Europe is less and less ready to accept refugees, yet they cannot all stay in Turkey. Meanwhile the situation in Syria is growing more and more hopeless, with no solution to the chaotic conflict presenting itself , and the threat of an all-out war growing daily.

What Is to Be Done?

So what is required in such a desperate situation? What should Europe do? Fredric Jameson recently proposed the utopia of the global militarization of society as a mode of emancipation: while the deadlocks of global capitalism are more and more palpable, all the imagined democratic-multitude-grassroots changes 'from below' are ultimately doomed to fail, so the only way to effectively break the vicious cycle of global capitalism is some kind of 'militarization', which is another name for suspending the power of the self-regulating economy.[56] Perhaps the ongoing refugee crisis in Europe provides an opportunity to test this option.

It is sheer madness to think that such a process can be left to unwind freely: if nothing else, refugees need provisions and medical care. One has to admit that in 2015 Germany demonstrated unexpected openness in accepting hundreds of thousands of refugees. (One wonders if the secret reason for this German magnanimity is not the need to wash away the bitter taste of how Greece was treated earlier in the same year.) What is needed to stop the chaos is large-scale coordination and organization: the establishment of reception centres close to the very core of the crisis (Turkey, Lebanon, the Syrian coast, the north African coast), where thousands have to be registered and scanned; the organized transport of those accepted to reception centres in Europe, and their redistribution to their potential sites of settlement. The military is the only agent that can undertake such a big task in an organized way. To claim that giving the military such a role smells of 'state of emergency' is simply hypocritical: a situation in which tens of thousands pass through densely populated areas without any organization is indeed a state of emergency, and parts of Europe are in one right now.

The criteria for acceptance and settlement have to be formulated in a clear and explicit way: which and how many refugees to accept, where to relocate them, and so on. The art here is to find the right middle way between following the desires of the refugees (taking into account their wish to move to countries where they already have relatives, etc.) and the capacities of different countries to accommodate them. The total right to 'free movement' should be limited, if for no other reason than that it doesn't exist even among the refugees: who – especially with regard to class position – is able to overcome all the obstacles and enter Europe is obviously a matter of financial privilege, among other things.[57]

Furthermore, it is a simple fact that most of the refugees come from a culture that is incompatible with Western European notions of human rights. The problem here is that the obviously tolerant solution (mutual respect of each other's sensitivities) no less obviously doesn't work. If Muslims find it impossible to bear our blasphemous images and reckless humour (which we consider a part of our freedoms), Western liberals also find it impossible to bear many practices (such as the subordination of women) that are part of the Muslim life-world. In short, situations explode when members of a religious community experience as blasphemous injury and a danger to their way of life not a direct attack on their religion, but the very way of life of another community: this was the case with attacks on gays and lesbians by Muslim fundamentalists in the Netherlands, Germany and Denmark, and with those Frenchmen and women who see a woman covered by a burka as an attack on their French identity, which is why they also find it 'impossible to remain silent' when they encounter such a woman in their midst. One has therefore to do two things: first, formulate a minimum set of norms that are obligatory for everyone, without fear that they will appear 'Eurocentric': religious freedoms, the protection of individual freedom against group pressure, rights of women, and so on; and second, within these limits, unconditionally insist on the toleration of different ways of life. And what if norms and communication don't work? Then the force of law should be applied in all its forms. One should reject the predominant Left-liberal humanitarian attitude. Complaints that moralize the situation – the mantras of 'Europe has lost empathy; it is indifferent towards the suffering of others,' and so on – are merely the obverse of racist anti-immigrant brutality. They share the presupposition – which is in no way self-evident – that a defence of one's own way of life excludes ethical universalism.

In the debate about *Leitkultur* (the dominant culture) that took place around a decade ago, conservatives insisted that every state is based on a predominant cultural space, which the members of other cultures living in the same space should respect. Instead of playing the Beautiful Soul and bemoaning the emergence of a new European racism that is heralded by such statements, we should turn a critical eye upon ourselves, asking to what extent our own abstract multiculturalism has contributed to this sad state of affairs. If all sides do not share or respect the same civility, then multiculturalism turns into a form of legally regulated mutual ignorance or hatred. The conflict about multiculturalism already *is* a conflict about *Leitkultur*: it is not a conflict between cultures, but a conflict between different visions of how different cultures can and should co-exist; about the rules and practices these cultures have to share if they are to co-exist. One should therefore avoid getting caught up in the liberal game of 'how much tolerance can we afford': should we tolerate it if refugees settling in Europe prevent their children going to school; if they force their women to dress and behave in a certain way; if they arrange the marriages of their children, if they maltreat – and worse – gays among their ranks? At this level, of course, we are never tolerant enough; or we are always-already too tolerant, neglecting the rights of women, and so on. The only way to break out of this deadlock is to move beyond mere tolerance of others. Don't just respect others: offer them a common struggle, since our problems today are common; propose and fight for a positive universal project shared by all participants.[58]

This is why the crucial task of those fighting for emancipation today is towards a positive emancipatory *Leitkultur*, which alone can sustain an authentic coexistence and immixing of different cultures. Our axiom should be that the struggle against Western neocolonialism as well as the struggle against fundamentalism, the struggle of Wikileaks and Snowden as well as the struggle of Pussy Riot, the struggle against anti-Semitism as well as the struggle against aggressive Zionism, are parts of one and the same universal struggle. If we make any compromise here, if we are lost in pragmatic compromises, our lives are not worth living.

One has therefore to broaden the perspective: refugees are the price humanity is paying for the global economy. While large migrations are a constant feature of human history, their main cause, in modern history, is colonial expansions. Prior to colonization, countries mostly consisted of self-sufficient and relatively isolated local communities: it was colonial occupation that threw off the rails this traditional way of life and which led to large-scale migrations (not, of course, forgetting the other related forced migrations of the slave trade).

The ongoing wave of migrations in Europe is no exception to this. In South Africa, over a million refugees from Zimbabwe are exposed to violence from the local poor for 'stealing' their jobs. And there will be more migrations, not just because of armed conflicts, but because of new 'rogue states', economic crises, natural disasters, climate change, and so on. It is now known that, after the Fukushima nuclear disaster of 2011, Japanese authorities thought for a moment that the entire Tokyo area – 20 million people – might have to be evacuated. Where, in this case, would they have gone? Under what conditions? Would they be given a piece of land in Japan on which to settle, or be dispersed around the world? What if northern Siberia were to become more inhabitable and appropriate for agriculture, while large sub-Saharan regions grow too arid to sustain large populations: how would such an exchange of population be organized? When similar things happened in the past, social changes occurred in a chaotic and spontaneous way, accompanied by violence and destruction. Such a prospect is catastrophic in today's conditions, with weapons of mass destruction available to virtually all nations.

The main lesson to be learned, therefore, is that humankind should get ready to live in a more 'plastic' and nomadic way: local or global changes in environment may result in the need for unheard-of large-scale social transformations and population movements. We are all more or less rooted in a particular way of life, protected by rights, but some historical contingency may all of a sudden throw us into a situation in which we are compelled to reinvent the basic coordinates of our way of life. (It seems that even today, centuries after the arrival of white men, Native Americans ('Indians') haven't succeeded in stabilizing their situation in a new way of life.) One thing is clear: in cases of such turmoil, national sovereignty will have to be radically redefined and new levels of global cooperation invented. And what about the immense economic and consumer changes that will have to happen as a result of new weather patterns or shortages of water and energy sources? Through what decision-making processes will such changes be agreed on and executed? The solution is not some mythic 'freedom of movement for all', but a carefully prepared and well-organized process of change.

Europe will have to reassert its full commitment to providing means for the dignified survival of refugees. There should be no compromise here. Large migrations are our future, and the only alternative to such commitments is a renewed barbarism (or what some will call the 'clash of civilizations'). However, the most difficult and important task is a radical economic change that abolishes the conditions that create refugees. The ultimate cause of refugees is today's global capitalism itself and its geopolitical games. If we do not transform it radically, immigrants from Greece and other European countries will soon join African refugees.

When I was young, such an organized attempt to regulate the commons was called Communism. Maybe we should reinvent it. It is not enough to remain faithful to the Communist Idea: one has to locate in historical reality the antagonisms that make this Idea a practical urgency. The only *true* question today is this: do we endorse the predominant acceptance of capitalism as a fact of (human) nature, or does today's global capitalism contain strong enough antagonisms to prevent its indefinite reproduction? There are in fact four such antagonisms: the looming threat of ecological catastrophe; the more and more palpable failure of *private property* to integrate into its functioning so-called 'intellectual property'; the socio-ethical implications of new techno-scientific developments (especially in biogenetics); and, last but not least, as has been mentioned above, new forms of apartheid, new walls and slums. There is a qualitative difference between the last feature, the gap that separates the Excluded from the Included, and the other three, which designate the domains of what Michael Hardt and Toni Negri call 'commons', the shared substance of our social being whose privatization is a violent act which should also be resisted, with violent means if necessary. These domains are:

– *the commons of culture*, the immediately socialized forms of 'cognitive' capital, primarily language – our means of communication and education – but also the shared infrastructure of public transport, electricity, mail, etc. (If Bill Gates were to be allowed a monopoly, we would have reached the absurd situation in which a private individual had literally taken ownership of the software texture of our basic network of communication);

– *the commons of external nature*, threatened by pollution and exploitation (from oil to forests and the natural habitat itself);

– *the commons of internal nature* (the biogenetic inheritance of humanity): with new biogenetic technology, the creation of a New Man in the literal sense of changing human nature becomes a realistic prospect.

What the struggles to defend these commons share is an awareness of the destructive potential that may be unleashed if the capitalist logic of enclosing the commons is allowed free reign, perhaps resulting in the self-annihilation of humanity itself. It is this reference to 'commons' that justifies the resuscitation of the notion of Communism: it enables us to see the progressive 'enclosure' of the commons as a process of proletarianization of those who are thereby excluded from their own substance. However, commons can also be restored to collective humanity without Communism, in an authoritarian-communitarian regime: the de-substantialized, 'rootless' subject, deprived of its substantial content, can also be counteracted in the direction of communitarianism, of finding its proper place in a new substantial community. There is nothing more 'private' than a state community that perceives the Excluded as a threat and worries how to keep them at a proper distance. In other words, in the series of four antagonisms outlined above, the one between the Included and the Excluded is the crucial one: without it, all others lose their subversive edge. Ecology turns into a problem of sustainable development; intellectual property into a complex legal challenge; biogenetics into an ethical issue. One can sincerely fight for ecology, defend a broader notion of intellectual property, oppose the copyrighting of genes, without confronting the antagonism between the Included and the Excluded: one can even formulate some of these struggles in the terms of the Included threatened by the polluting Excluded. In this way, we get no true universality, only 'private' concerns in the Kantian sense of the term. Corporations like Whole Foods and Starbucks continue to enjoy favour among liberals even though they both engage in anti-union activities. The trick is that they sell products with a progressive spin: one buys coffee made with beans bought at above fair-market value, one drives a hybrid vehicle, one buys from companies that provide good benefits for their customers (according to the corporation's own standards), and so on. In short, without the antagonism between the Included and the Excluded, we may well find ourselves in a world in which Bill Gates is the greatest humanitarian fighting against poverty and disease, and Rupert Murdoch the greatest environmentalist, mobilizing hundreds of millions through his media empire.

It is at this point that refugees – those from the Outside that want to penetrate the Inside – bear witness to another level of the endangered commons: the commons of humanity itself, threatened by a global capitalism which generates new walls and other forms of apartheid. Only the fourth antagonism, the reference to the Excluded, justifies the term Communism: the first three effectively concern questions of humanity's economic, anthropological, even physical survival, while the fourth one is ultimately a question of justice.

So who will do all this? Who will be the agent of the restoration of the commons? There is only one correct answer to Leftist intellectuals desperately awaiting the arrival of a new revolutionary agent, the old Hopi saying with a wonderful Hegelian dialectical twist from substance to subject: 'We are the ones we have been waiting for.' (This saying is a version of Gandhi's motto, 'Be yourself the change you want to see in the world.') Waiting for another to do the job for us is a way of rationalizing our inactivity. However, the trap to be avoided here is the one of perverse self-instrumentalization: 'We are the ones we are waiting for' does not mean that we have to discover how *we* are the agent predestined by fate (historical necessity) to do the task. It means, on the contrary, that there is no big Other to rely on. In contrast to classical Marxism, in which 'history is on our side' (the proletariat fulfils a predestined task of universal emancipation), in today's constellation, the big Other is *against* us: left to itself, the inner thrust of our historical development leads to catastrophe, to apocalypse. Here, the only thing that can prevent catastrophe is *pure voluntarism*, i.e. our free decision to act against historical necessity. In a way, it was the Bolsheviks who, towards the end of the civil war in 1921, found themselves in a similar predicament. Two years before his death, when it became clear that there would be no all-European revolution, and remembering that the idea of building socialism in one country was nonsense, Lenin wrote:

> What if the complete hopelessness of the situation, by stimulating the efforts of the workers and peasants tenfold, offered us the opportunity to create the fundamental requisites of civilization in a different way from that of the West European countries?[59]

Giorgio Agamben observed that 'thought is the courage of hopelessness'[60] – an insight which is especially pertinent for our historical moment, when even the most pessimistic diagnoses as a rule finish with an uplifting hint at some version of the proverbial light at the end of the tunnel. The true courage is not to imagine an alternative, but to accept the consequences of the fact that there is no clearly discernible alternative. The dream of an alternative is a sign of theoretical cowardice: it functions as a fetish that prevents us thinking to the end the deadlock of our predicament. In short, the truly courageous stance is to admit that the light at the end of the tunnel is most probably the headlight of a train approaching us from the opposite direction.

Is this not the predicament of the Morales government in Bolivia, or of the (now deposed) Aristide government in Haiti and the Maoist government in Nepal, or of the Syriza government in Greece? Their situation is 'objectively' hopeless. The whole drift of history is basically against them: they cannot rely on any 'objective tendencies' pushing them on their way. All they can do is to improvise, do what they can in a desperate situation. But, nonetheless, does this not give them a unique freedom? One is tempted to apply here the old distinction between 'freedom from' and 'freedom for': does their freedom from History (with its laws and objective tendencies) not sustain their freedom for creative experimenting? In their actions, they can rely only on the collective will of their supporters.

Maybe this is, in the long term, our only solution. Is all this a utopia? Maybe, even probably. The latest chaotic events in Europe, the half-tragic half-comical mixture of impotent declarations and chaotic-egotistic behaviour of the EU members, the inability to impose a minimum of coordinated action, demonstrates not only a particular failure of the EU but a threat to its very survival. The Leftist counterpoint to this confusion is an idea circulating in the underground of many disappointed radical Leftists, a softer repetition of the decision for terror in the aftermath of the 1968 movement: the crazy idea that only a radical catastrophe (preferably an ecological one) can awaken the large crowds and in doing so give a new impetus to radical emancipation. The latest version of this idea relates to the refugees: only an influx of a really large number of refugees (and their disappointment since, obviously, Europe will not be able to satisfy their expectations) can revitalize the European radical Left . . . I find this line of thought obscene: notwithstanding the fact that such a development would for sure give an immense boost to anti-immigrant brutality, the truly crazy aspect of this idea is the project to replenish the ranks of missing radical proletarians in Europe by importing them from abroad, so that we will thereby bring about revolution by an imported revolutionary agent . . .

During the first half of 2015, Europe was preoccupied by radical emancipatory movements (Syriza, Podemos), while in the second half the attention has shifted to the 'humanitarian' topic of the refugees: a shift in which class struggle was literally repressed and replaced by liberal-cultural notions of tolerance and solidarity. With the Paris terror killings on Friday 13 November, however, even these ideas (which at least still involve large socio-economic issues) are now eclipsed by the simple opposition of all democratic forces caught in a merciless war with forces of terror – and it is easy to imagine what will follow: the paranoiac search for ISIS agents among the refugees, and so on. The greatest victims of the Paris terror attacks will be refugees themselves, and the true winners, concealed behind the platitudes in the style of *je suis Paris*, will be simply the partisans of total war on both sides. This is how we should *really* condemn the Paris killings: not by engaging in pathetic shows of anti-terrorist solidarity but by insisting on asking one simple question: *cui bono*? And there should be no 'deeper understanding' of the ISIS terrorists (in the sense of 'their deplorable acts are nonetheless reactions to brutal European interventions'): they should be characterized as what they are, as the Islamo-Fascist obverse of the European anti-immigrant racists – the two are two sides of the same coin.

So let's bring class struggle back – and the only way to do it is to insist on the global solidarity of the exploited and oppressed. Without this global view, the pathetic solidarity with Paris victims is a pseudo-ethical obscenity. Although a great obscurity surrounds the influx of refugees into Europe, the majority of them undoubtedly are trying to escape terrifying conditions in their country. A day after the Paris attacks, one of them dryly commented on TV: 'Imagine a city like Paris, where the state of exception that reigns there today is simply a permanent feature of daily life for months if not for years. This is what we are escaping from.' One cannot ignore the moment of truth in this statement: don't confuse terrorists and their victims.

Maybe such global solidarity is a utopia. But if we don't engage in it, then we are really lost. And we will deserve to be lost.

Notes

1. http://www.theguardian.com/commentisfree/2015/nov/18/turkey-cut-islamic-state-supply-lines-erdogan-isis.

2. Peter Sloterdijk, *In the World Interior of Capital*, Cambridge: Polity Press, 2013, p. 8.

3. Ibid., p. 9.

4. Ibid.

5. Ibid.

6. Quoted from http://www.lrb.co.uk/v37/n22/jacqueline-rose/bantu-in-the-bathroom.

7. For a detailed critical analysis of mainstream liberal feminism, see Nancy Fraser, *Fortunes of Feminism*, London: Verso Books, 2013.

8. Quoted from https://www.marxists.org/reference/archive/wilde-oscar/soul-man/.

9. Quoted from http://www.independent.co.uk/voices/i-didnt-think-ttip-could-get-any-scarier-but-then-i-spoke-to-the-eu-official-in-charge-of-it-a6690591.html.

10. See Jeremy Rifkin's *The Age of Access*, New York: JP Tarcher, 2001. Along similar lines, Gerhard Schulze proposed the concept of *Erlebnisgesellschaft*, the 'society of [lived] experience', in which the dominant norms are those of pleasure and quality of life-experiences – see Gerhard Schulze, *Die Erlebnisgesellschaft. Kultursoziologie der Gegenwart*, Frankfurt and New York: Campus Verlag, 1992.

11. Quoted from Rifkin, op. cit., p. 171.

12. Epigraph of 'Living Room Dialogues on the Middle East', quoted from Wendy Brown, *Regulating Aversion*, Princeton: Princeton University Press, 2006.

13. Incidentally, the same PC Leftist liberals who practise a super-hermeneutics of suspicion apropos Western societies, discerning traces of sexism or racism in the barely perceptible details of our speech and behaviour, display breathtaking tolerance when confronted with women wearing a burka, seeing in it playful forms of resistance, an act of anti-commodification (a protest against the reduction of women to sexual objects), etc. – there is, of course, a moment of truth in all this, but it doesn't change the fact that the burka's basic meaning is to enact woman's subordination.

14. Numbers in brackets refer to pages in Talal Asad, Wendy Brown, Judith Butler and Saba Mahmood, *Is Critique Secular?*, Berkeley: University of California Press, 2009.

15. See http://gawker.com/orthodox-jews-invent-uber-for-protesting-gay-pride-1714720843.

16. Quoted from http://www.christianexaminer.com/article/israeli-foreign-minister-bible-says-the-land-is-ours/49013.htm.

17. For the violent dark side of Buddhism, see Brian Victoria, *Zen War Stories*, London: Routledge, 2003, as well as *Buddhist Warfare*, ed. Michael Jerryson and Mark Juergensmeyer, Oxford: Oxford University Press, 2010.

18. For the quotations in this paragraph, see http://www.theguardian.com/world/2015/oct/21/netanyahu-under-fire-for-palestinian-grand-mufti-holocaust-claim.

19. Quoted from http://www.independent.co.uk/news/uk/crime/rotherham-child-abuse-the-victims-stories-doused-with-petrol-and-told-she-would-be-set-alight-9692577.html. I rely on this report also for my other data about the Rotherham scandal.

20. In what follows I refer to many comments in the *Guardian, Independent*, etc., which can be easily found via Google.

21. See Sergio González Rodríguez, *The Femicide Machine*, Los Angeles: Semiotext(e), 2012.

22. See *Forsaken: The Report of the Missing Women Commission of Inquiry*, by Wally T. Oppal, Commissioner, British Columbia, 19 November 2012, available online at http://www.missing womeninquiry.ca/wp-content/uploads/2010/10/Forsaken-ES-web-RGB.pdf.

23. See http://www.theglobeandmail.com/news/national/verdict-in-death-of-indigenous-sex-worker-sparks-rallies-calls-for-appeal/article23651385/.

24. 'Critique of Violence', in Walter Benjamin, *Reflections*, New York: Schocken Books, 1986, p. 294.

25. See Guy le Gaufey, *Une archéologie de la toute-puissance*, Paris: Epel, 2014, p. 74.

26. I obtained this passage from Sami Khatib (Berlin), who is preparing the English translation of Kraft's diaries.

27. Ruth Klüger, *Still Alive: A Holocaust Girlhood Remembered*, New York: The Feminist Press, 2003, p. 189.

28. Available online at www.cbsnews.com/stories/2008/10/23/world/main4542268.shtm.

29. Quoted from http://www.informationclearinghouse.info/article 42811.htm.

30. Ibid.

31. See http://www.nationalreview.com/article/426046/human-smugglers-profit-syrian-refugee-crisis.

32. See https://horseedmedia.net/2015/10/28/somalia-saudi-arabia-deports-over-100-somalis-to-mogadishu/.

33. See https://en.wikipedia.org/wiki/Saudi_Arabian_involvement_in_the_Syrian_Civil_War.

34. See Thomas Frank, *What's the Matter with Kansas? How Conservatives Won the Heart of America*, New York: Metropolitan Books, 2004.

35. See Ernesto Laclau and Chantal Mouffe, *Hegemony and Socialist Strategy*, London: Verso Books, 1985.

36. Jane Perlez and Pir Zubair Shah, 'Taliban Exploit Class Rifts in Pakistan', *New York Times*, 16 April 2009. The ideological bias in the article is nonetheless discernible, in the way that it speaks of the Taliban's 'ability to exploit class divisions', as if the 'true' Taliban agenda lies elsewhere – in religious fundamentalism – and that they are merely 'taking advantage' of the plight of the poor landless farmers. To this, one should simply add two things. First, such a distinction between a 'true' agenda and instrumental manipulation is externally imposed on the Taliban: as if the poor landless farmers themselves do not experience their plight in 'fundamentalist religious' terms! Second, if, by 'taking advantage' of the farmers' plight, the Taliban are 'raising alarm about the risks to Pakistan, which remains largely feudal', what prevents liberal democrats in Pakistan as well as the US from similarly 'taking advantage' of this plight and trying to help the landless farmers? The sad implication of the fact that this obvious question is not raised in the *New York Times* report is that the feudal forces in Pakistan are the 'natural ally' of liberal democracy . . .

37. Thomas Altizer, personal communication.

38. See http://inthesetimes.com/article/18425/why-the-radical-left-really-really-needs-to-quit-whining-about-bernie-sanders.

39. See, for example, Costas Douzinas, *Human Rights and Empire*, New York: Routledge, 2007.

40. Quoted from http://www.ibtimes.co.uk/zimbabwe-we-are-not-gays-president-robert-mugabe-rejects-homosexual-rights-un-speech-1521685.

41. See http://www.africaundisguised.com/newsportal/story/zimbabwe-president-says-homosexuals-are-worse-pigs-and-dogs.

42. Quoted from http://www.voxeurop.eu/en/content/news-brief/
2437991-orban-considers-alternative-democracy.

43. See http://dailycurrant.com/2015/09/07/sarah-palin-native-
americans-should-go-back-to-nativia-3/

44. Jacques Lacan, 'Proposition of 9 October 1967 on the Psycho-
analyst of the School', in *Analysis*, Issue 6 (1995), p. 12.

45. Peter Sloterdijk, 'Warten auf den Islam', *Focus*, 10 (2006), p. 84.

46. Robert Pippin, 'What Is a Western? Politics and Self-Knowledge
in John Ford's *The Searchers*', *Critical Inquiry*, Vol. 35, No. 2 (Win-
ter 2009), p. 240–41.

47. Alenka Zupančič, 'Locked Room Comedy' (unpublished essay
on Preston Sturges).

48. James Harvey, *Romantic Comedy in Hollywood. From Lubitsch to
Sturges*, New York: Knopff, 1987, p. 141.

49. See Alain Badiou, *Notre mal vient de plus loin*, Paris: Fayard, 2015.
(Numbers in brackets refer to pages in this book.)

50. Jean-Claude Milner, 'Rechtsstaat und Kalifat', *Lettre International*, 111, p. 19.

51. Jean-Jacques Rousseau, *Rousseau, Judge of Jean-Jacques: Dialogues*,
Hanover: Dartmouth College Press, 1990, p. 63.

52. See Jean-Pierre Dupuy, *Petite métaphysique des tsunamis*, Paris:
Éditions du Seuil, 2005, p. 68.

53. According to the Islamic State ideological narrative, 'Islam's
final showdown with an anti-Messiah will occur in Jerusalem
after a period of renewed Islamic conquest . . . An anti-Messiah,
known in Muslim apocalyptic literature as Dajjal, will come
from the Khorasan region of eastern Iran and kill a vast number of the caliphate's fighters, until just 5,000 remain, cornered
in Jerusalem. Just as Dajjal prepares to finish them off, Jesus –
the second-most-revered prophet in Islam – will return to
Earth, spear Dajjal, and lead the Muslims to victory' (http://

www.theatlantic.com/magazine/archive/2015/03/what-isis-really-wants/384980/). Sounds familiar? Of course: it is the slightly reformulated Armageddon story regularly used by American Christian fundamentalists . . . so good to see Christian and Muslim fundamentalists moving in the same direction and relying on the same ideological fantasies even when they pretend to hate each other.

54. Quoted from http://www.theguardian.com/world/2016/jan/05/germany-crisis-cologne-new-years-eve-sex-attacks.

55. Quoted from http://www.misterdann.com/earlyargreatcat-massacre.htm. The original source is Robert Darnton, *The Great Cat Massacre and Other Episodes in French Cultural History*, London: Basic Books, 2009. The following description is condensed from Darnton's book.

56. See Fredric Jameson, 'An American Utopia', in *An American Utopia: Dual Power and the Universal Army*, edited by Slavoj Žižek, London: Verso Books, 2016.

57. That's why, incidentally, Lenin, an internationalist if there ever was one, insisted on the importance of frontiers: 'What does the "method" of socialist revolution under the slogan "Down with frontiers" mean? We maintain that the state is necessary, and a state presupposes frontiers. The state, of course, may hold a bourgeois government, but we need the Soviets. But even Soviets are confronted with the question of frontiers. What does "Down with frontiers" mean? It is the beginning of anarchy [. . .] The "method" of socialist revolution under the slogan "Down with frontiers" is simply a mess. Only when the socialist revolution has become a reality, and not a method, will the slogan "Down with frontiers" be a correct slogan. Then we shall say: Comrades, come to us . . .' (Quoted from https://www.marxists. org/archive/lenin/works/1917/7thconf/29d.htm.)

58. The complex predicament of Tibet throughout the 1950s clearly shows the limitations of respect for a specific way of life (in this case, respect for the Tibetan feudal theocracy). In late 1950, a local farmer sought refuge with a Chinese Army garrison after local Tibetan authorities threatened to punish him severely for his 'illicit' (in view of the local feudal rules) act of visiting his relatives in a nearby village without asking for permission from his feudal master. After long deliberation, the Chinese army decided to give him protection – and was immediately accused by the Tibetan local powers of brutally intervening into their specific way of life . . .

59. V. I. Lenin, *Collected Works*, Vol. 33, Moscow: Progress Publishers, 1966, p. 479.

60. Quoted from http://www.versobooks.com/blogs/1612-thought-is-the-courage-of-hopelessness-an-interview-with-philosopher-giorgio-agamben.